Acknowledgments

I would like to thank the many artists and designers who allowed me to include their work in this edition. My sincere thanks to Margaret Cummins, senior editor at John Wiley & Sons, for agreeing to release a second edition and for her editorial help; Lauren Poplawski, senior editorial assistant, and Ava Wilder, senior production editor, for their production assistance; and Karin C. Warren for her help in developing the manuscript. I continue to learn from my students, to be inspired by my former art and design professors, and to be assisted by my colleagues and former graduate student classmates. Thank you all.

Special thanks to my wife Helene (a designer), my mother (a poet), my step-father (an engineer), and my late father (an artist) for their encouragement and inspiration.

Kurt Vonnegut once said that the secret to success in any creative activity is to do it with one person as your audience. I actually had two people in mind when I wrote this edition: my children, Jackson and Sofia.

Contents Introduction to Two-Dimensional Design

Introduction to Two-Dimensional Design: Understanding Form and Function
Second Edition

John Bowers

WILEY

John Wiley & Sons, Inc.

Published by John Wiley & Sons, Inc., Hoboken, New Jersey
Published simultaneously in Canada

For general information about our other products and services, please contact our
Customer Care Department within the United States at (800) 762-2974, outside the
United States at (317) 572-3993 or fax (317) 572-4002.

Wiley also publishes its books in a variety of electronic formats. Some content that
appears in print may not be available in electronic books. For more information
about Wiley products, visit our web site at www.wiley.com.

Library of Congress Cataloging-in-Publication Data:

Bowers, John, 1959-
  Introduction to two-dimensional design: understanding form and function/
John Bowers.—2nd ed.
    p. cm.
  Includes bibliographical references and index.
  ISBN 978-0-470-16375-7 (pbk.)
  1. Design. I. Title.
  NC703.B68 2008
  760—dc22   2007051392

Printed in the United States of America

10 9 8 7 6

Contents

Introduction to Two-Dimensional Design: Understanding Form and Function
Second Edition

John Bowers

WILEY

John Wiley & Sons, Inc.

This book is printed on acid-free paper. ⊚

Copyright © 2008 by John Wiley & Sons, Inc. All rights reserved

Published by John Wiley & Sons, Inc., Hoboken, New Jersey
Published simultaneously in Canada

For general information about our other products and services, please contact our
Customer Care Department within the United States at (800) 762-2974, outside the
United States at (317) 572-3993 or fax (317) 572-4002.

Wiley also publishes its books in a variety of electronic formats. Some content that
appears in print may not be available in electronic books. For more information
about Wiley products, visit our web site at www.wiley.com.

Library of Congress Cataloging-in-Publication Data:

Bowers, John, 1959-
  Introduction to two-dimensional design: understanding form and function/
John Bowers.—2nd ed.
    p. cm.
  Includes bibliographical references and index.
  ISBN 978-0-470-16375-7 (pbk.)
1. Design. I. Title.
NC703.B68 2008
  760—dc22   2007051392

Printed in the United States of America

10 9 8 7 6

Introduction

0.1
"Visit UnCity," 1972
Designer Unknown

I was 12 years old when I purchased my first billboard. It was the early 1970s, when the soft drink 7UP was being promoted as the Uncola. The 7UP campaign included billboards that you could buy directly from the company. I remember placing an order for a billboard titled "Visit UnCity" and waiting impatiently for it to arrive.

I still have that billboard today. When I first saw it I wasn't aware of the marketing strategy behind it or the social conditions that inspired its design. I was simply taken with its beauty, playfulness, and size.

That billboard still has a mysterious hold over me, more than 35 years later. Some aspects of design are largely mysterious, and should be accepted as such, including the innate and lasting responses to imagery. But the ability to create emotional responses from imagery, to shape decision making through visual messages, and to develop and express personal and collective issues can be discussed, if not learned and applied.

This book demonstrates and explains how a design is shaped by its audience, content, context, and purpose, and conversely, how a design shapes interpretation through the use of media, agenda, and strategy.

The book begins with an overview of the origins, issues, and functions of design and goes on to describe the important theories and methods of creating and disseminating visual messages. It then identifies and describes visual components and principles common to two-dimensional design and culminates with an in-depth discussion of select individuals and collaborations whose work exemplifies the book's discussions.

The book illustrates some of the commonalities among non-applied (largely fine art) and applied (largely graphic design) activities. It addresses activities or concerns of a personal nature, such as artists' books, as well as activities of a non-personal nature or those disseminated on a large scale to targeted audiences, such as visual identity systems. For convenience and because I believe that non-applied and applied activities have much in common, I use the word *design* to describe both in broad terms.

Accompanying the discussion in each chapter are visual examples by recognized and contemporary artists and designers, as well as works by lesser known or emerging artists and even by some without formal education. This variety demonstrates the broad nature of design problems and solutions.

The "Visit UnCity" billboard that so entranced me as a boy is a reflection of a cultural moment in time. Design offers an opportunity to create long-lasting inspiration, to foster meaningful communication, and to express social change. It carries with it immense social responsibility. I hope this book will help you explore these and the many other aspects of design.

Thinking Broadly

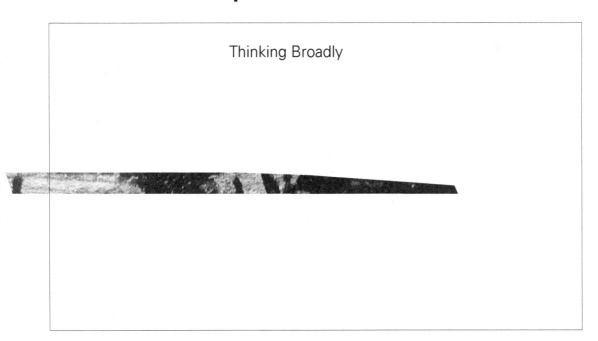

Concepts

Sources
Activities
Origins
Influences
Issues

Roles
Form
Function
Experiences
Voice

This chapter discusses how we as designers, viewers, and users are participants in the creation and evaluation of visual messages. It examines how design both influences and is influenced by culture.

Thinking Broadly

1.1
Planet Earth

We are a place of 6.6 billion inhabitants, 250 languages, and 245 sovereign states.

"Every human being is a designer."[1]

Norman Potter

Every day, we process information, organize objects, filter opinions, act on opportunities, and physically create things. We design our space, our interactions, and our future.

Design is a form of expression and communication. It also provides a way to organize our environment, understand relationships, shape routines, and derive meaning.

The word *design* is both a noun and a verb: it is a product of thinking and an extension of thinking. The word has its roots in the Italian verb *disegnare*, which means to create. Whether understood as a noun, a verb, or both, design is all around us: in human-made and natural forms and in the ways we communicate with and understand one another and our environment.

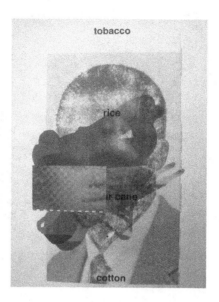

1.2
Chattel #1, 1995
Frank DeBose

DeBose's ancestral experience of slavery is explored in self-portraits that layer related imagery to heighten awareness of the issue.

Design is a form's visual appearance, message, and purpose. In a broad sense, this includes its context, targeted audience, and media, which collectively describe its form and function. Design can be applied (such as graphic design) or non-applied (such as fine art).

Design encompasses many types of activities. Design that communicates specific ideas for targeted audiences, design generated out of personal experience, and design of broad social value are among the many areas this book explores.

Design crosses many disciplines, including the social sciences, business, and literature. In the broadest sense, design encompasses not only visual explorations, but also those cultural, social, and philosophical in nature.

1.3
Markings, AD 900–1200
Newspaper Rock, Arizona

Early drawings aided in the search for meaning. Anthropologists have found that early cultures rarely created art for pleasure alone due to their focus on survival.

Purpose refers to a design's goal or guiding principles and can be determined by an agenda, objective, or strategy.

Context refers to the physical location or cultural environment in which a work exists and influences the viewer's or user's interpretation of the work's message or function. For example, the letter X on a sidewalk may designate an excavation site for a public utility; on a greeting card it may represent a kiss and an expression of affection (e.g., XOXO); and on a shopping list it may indicate that an item was found.

As humans, we have basic, practical needs that must be met to sustain life. At a minimum, we require food, water, and shelter. We also have varying degrees of emotional and personal needs, including the desire to pursue and find meaning, self-fulfillment, and a sense of security.

Design often originates from basic human needs and desires. Since early recorded history, humans have sought to co-exist with and, at times, control others and the human-made and natural environment. Visual form and message-making is a primary way that we express our view of ourselves, others, and the world.

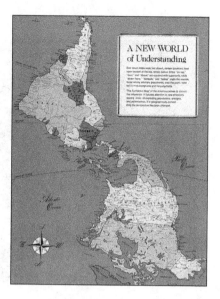

1.4
Upside-Down Map, 1982
Jessie Levine

This work comments on the mapping convention in which north is aligned at the top and east to the right. Early maps drawn by northerners positioned better-known regions in the upper-right corner for more convenient study.

Idea is an image or thought formed in the mind. Ideation is the process of forming and relating ideas.

Concept is an idea that serves as the basis of a work. All work has an underlying concept that is open to interpretation, whether ambiguous, obscure, or self-evident.

Design is influenced by a range of forces. A design initiated by an individual can be further influenced by others on a development team and by external forces. Marketing strategies, community regulatory codes, project deadlines and budgets, the methodology and technology employed to create the work, social or cultural conventions, and even accepted styles of the moment contribute to a work's visual appearance, delivery, and audience interpretation.

1.5
Advertisements for
United Colors of Benetton, 1992
O. Toscani,
United Colors of Benetton

Part of a series of advertisements
that used powerful imagery of
human tragedy as a means to sell
clothing while raising consciousness
about social issues.

Aesthetics is a branch of
philosophy that examines
the nature of sensory
perception and the experience
and definition of beauty.

Design is largely driven by the need or desire to address
a specific or broad set of issues. These issues can range
from private to public concerns such as developing a sense
of place, individual and collective responsibilities such
as those surrounding sustainability, and official and
unofficial actions such as those related to activism. These
issues can further range from the cultural or social to the
philosophical or ethical.

In this light, design is much more than the creation of
objects for beauty alone. Instead, design is used to inform
others, question conventions, create change, and promote
justice. As designers, we not only serve as transmitters
of messages, but also as interpreters and mediators.
More than makers, observers, or controllers of information
and ideas, designers are participants in the creation,
criticism, and dissemination of culture.

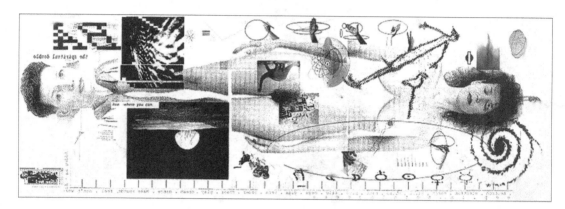

1.6
Does It Make Sense?
1985
April Greiman

One of the first digitally created graphic works, Greiman's full-size self-portrait uses her body to structure dream imagery, poetic text, and a time line of significant personal and world events.

Form has numerous meanings, many derived from the Latin word *forma*, which is based on the Greek words for shape, structure, and idea.

Concepts become tangible through form. Form is composed of visual components including lines, shapes, images, and colors. These components can be organized through principles such as visual hierarchy and emphasis, and developed through methodologies that help direct working processes, such as problem solving.

1.7
The Flooded Grave,
1998–2000
Jeff Wall

Wall's large-scale, back-lit photographs reveal the irony and contradiction of seemingly mundane scenes.

Function is a form's practical, spiritual, cultural, or personal use. In two-dimensional design, function is synonymous with purpose, with a form's intent. This includes an evaluation of why the form was created, its audience, how it will be used, and what it will do.

Every form has primary and secondary functions. Function is obvious in some forms. A saw, for example, has the mechanical function of dividing pieces of wood.

In two-dimensional form, function can be more abstract and difficult to define. A painting has no mechanical function, yet it can inspire, inform, or move us to action.

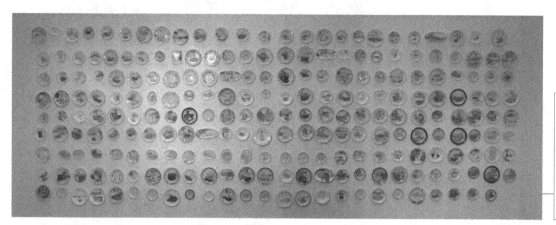

For a closer look, see Chapter 7

1.8
The Last Supper:
Final Meal Requests of
U.S. Death Row Inmates, 2006
Julie Green

Green explores last rites and requests
in the design of plates that show the last
meals of convicts before execution.

"As designers, we are
late in recognizing the fact
that representations
of differences in terms of
class, race, gender and
sexuality are constructed
through design."[2]

Garland Kirkpatrick

"To be successful, designers
must appreciate and reconcile
multiple viewpoints about
the same topic."[3]

Meredith Davis and Robin Moore

Designers are the creators of experiences. These experiences
can involve interactions or environments that shape a
moment or series of encounters, which in turn can create a
lasting impression or desired response. Building a sense of
participation, ownership, or loyalty to an idea is often
a design goal.

Experiences are often emotional in some way and attempt
to personalize the subject matter. From coffee retailers that
promote coffee as a lifestyle to political debates in which
candidates discuss social issues by relating stories of
their upbringing through emotional storytelling, experience
building is part of a larger cultural phenomenon.

"I was born in Oxford on April 1, 1910. My father
said I was the most beautiful baby in the most beautiful
state, so he named me Iowa."[4]
Iowa Honn

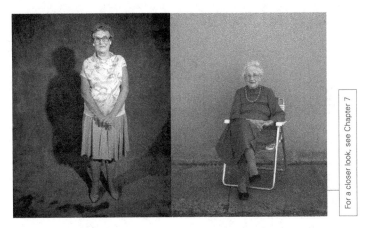

For a closer look, see Chapter 7

1.9
Iowa Honn, 1984 and 2004
Peter Feldstein, photographer
Steven Bloom, writer

Feldstein explores the lives of residents in
small-town Iowa, where he has photographed
over the past 20 years. His work brings
to light the hope and the losses of a tight-
knit community.

Interpretation is the translation
of a form's message through
the filter of one's perspective.
Interpretation derives meaning
and understanding.

Meaning is derived intent,
purpose, or information of
a message, and is influenced
by the viewer's or user's
experiences and abilities.

Voice is the combination of
unique perspective and
individual expression. It refers
to the choice and use of visual
principles and media, and to the
methods employed in presenting
ideas, desires, and opinions.

As designers, we have a unique role in society in that we
shape both the physical and cultural landscape. Through the
forms and messages we create and respond to, we define
who we are individually and collectively.

Design can illuminate difficult and complex issues, share the
plight of the marginalized, and allow reflection through the
creation of elegance and beauty. Every design function
has its time and place. Work that is memorable, has a degree
of originality, and that merges form and function creates
value on many levels.

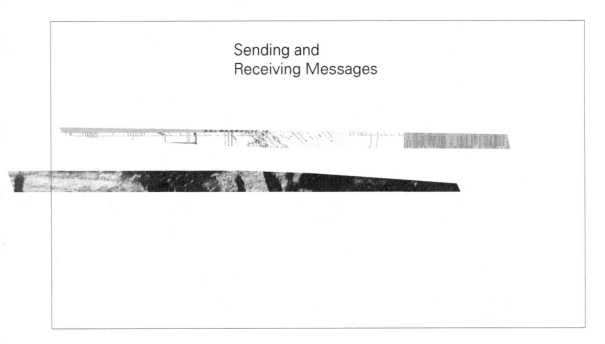

Sending and Receiving Messages

Concepts

Theory
Function
Communication Spaces
Contemporary Thinkers
Lens of Interpretation

Content
Themes
Value

Dissemination
Alphabets and Writing

Interactions
Audience and Place
Technology

Methods
Signals and Cues
Narratives and Storytelling

Representation
Symbolism and Imagery
Metaphors and Analogies

This chapter examines communication through the theoretical, technical, and cultural influences that shape how messages are sent, received, and interpreted.

Sending and Receiving Messages

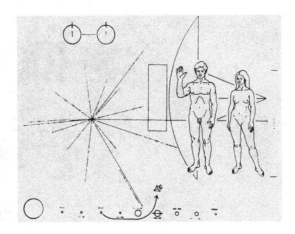

2.1
Plaque aboard Pioneer 10,
launched July 4, 1976
Frank Drake, Carl Sagan, and
Linda Sagan, designers

This plaque includes symbols signifying the
Earth's position in the solar system, the
origin of Pioneer 10, and representations of
humankind.

**"Design is the process by
which a designer creates
a context to be encountered
by a participant, from which
meaning emerges."**[5]

Katie Salen and Eric Zimmerman

Forms and messages are shaped by theories and created
through methodologies. These are aids to critically approach-
ing and understanding design. Through our experiences and
values, we interpret messages and derive meaning.

The theories and methodologies that influence design come
from many disciplines, including the humanities and social
sciences. They can direct how we see, interact, process, and
respond to forms and messages.

All messages are mediated, that is, to some extent messages
are led by individual or collective agendas; directed by
economic, political, or other strategies; and shaped
by the technologies used to create and disseminate them.
No message is without a point of view. Messages can also
be situated: the cultural context or physical location in which
they are presented influences our understanding of their
purpose and goal.

2.2
Billboard, 2001
Portland, Oregon

Public messages often promote and juxtapose the imagined over the real.

Theory describes groupings of ideas that seek to explain a phenomenon, guide investigation, or shape interpretation.

Theory helps us understand and interpret phenomena such as how we communicate with others or the ways we view imagery. Theory is based on a belief usually rooted in observation, analysis, evaluation, and factual information, and sometimes in feelings, past experiences, or hunches. Theory both describes and predicts a usable method of working and outcome, and is particularly relevant in applied design activity through which a form is disseminated to a broad audience.

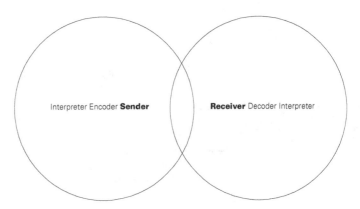

Interpreter Encoder **Sender**   **Receiver** Decoder Interpreter

2.3
Communication model

Contemporary models of communication emphasize the connection between sender and receiver, suggesting the two share roles as interpreters.

"The same sign may have different meanings to two people, or may have some meaning for one person and no meaning for another."[6]

Werner J. Severin
and James W. Tankard, Jr.

Audience refers to the receiver(s) of a message. An audience can be targeted or open-ended, narrow or broad, and treated as passive observers or active participants.

The word communication comes from the Latin word *communicare*, which means "to make common." Communication involves a sender and a receiver, a message, a medium, and a shared understanding of basic elements including words and symbols.

Communication is a science, as evidenced by research and theory that explores the processes involved. It is also a creative act, in that a given message can be sent or interpreted differently. When we communicate, we cannot be certain that a message will be understood, especially when communicating to persons from other cultures. We each have biases, experiences, and different educational backgrounds that influence how we process and act upon messages.

Modernism Late 1890s to present

Structuralism
Examination of structural components and relationships that yield meaning
Ferdinand de Saussure

Semiotics
Examination of signs (signifiers) and the process of determining meaning
Roland Barthes

Post-Modernism 1960s to present

Post-Structuralism
Examination of embedded codes as a way of expanding interpretation
Michel Foucault

Deconstruction
Examination of embedded opposites as a way of deriving multiple meanings
Jacques Derrida

U.S. Department of Transportation
sign (top)
Front and back covers from
The Portrait Series, 1996 (bottom)
Warren Lehrer

2.4
Select contemporary thought

Over the past century, theories from disciplines in philosophy and literature in particular have played a significant role in design. These theories have influenced visual appearances and the role of the audience in interpreting meaning.

Literary theory, which explores language, roles of the reader, and modes of presentation, has fostered a move from guided experiences that are visually structured to guided experiences less visually structured or singular in meaning. For example, rather than information presented in a linear, top-to-bottom, left-to-right, hierarchical format, presentation has shifted toward the non-linear, as experienced in interactive media.

Underlying this visual shift is increased audience participation, from (at times) passive to active. Contemporary work often asks the viewer or user to decode and connect seemingly unrelated imagery.

Theory Lens of Interpretation

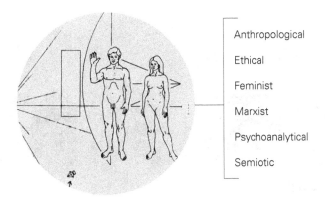

2.5
Detail of Pioneer 10 plaque

Select contemporary viewpoints for critiquing messages.

Anthropological critiques might ask, how is a message an expression of a ritual or place?

Ethical critiques might ask, what are the social implications of a message?

Feminist critiques might ask, how does a message support equality or further stereotypes?

Marxist critiques might ask, under what economic conditions is a message created and disseminated, and what and whose goals does it support?

Psychoanalytical critiques might ask, what is the subjective value and outcome of experiencing a message?

Semiotic critiques might ask, what purpose does a message support?

Whether consciously or subconsciously, we each view messages through a viewpoint (or lens). The lens can be anthropological, ethical, feminist, Marxist, psychoanalytical, semiotic—or any variation or combination of these and other disciplines or modes of thought.

Depending on the lens used, forms and messages can yield multiple and even competing meanings. In addition, meaning itself is often unstable; it can change over time and be influenced by the physical location and cultural setting in which a message is viewed. What constitutes ethical behavior, for example, is open to interpretation and shaped by cultural conventions and codes.

Content Themes

2.6
Select images of the
High Water Line Project, 2007
Eve S. Mosher

2.7
Mudflap Lady,
2006
Margo Gradjea

2.8
The Book of Lies,
2007
Warren Lehrer

2.9
*Do Women Have to Be Naked to
Get into the Metropolitan Museum?*
Venice Bienniale installation, 2005
Guerrilla Girls

Place is a theme embedded in the work of Eve S. Mosher. A white chalk line was drawn through lower Manhattan to mark impending rising water levels due to global warming.

Identity is a theme explored by Margo Gradjea, who questions the message and value of cultural icons, including the female depiction commonly seen on the mud flaps of semi-trucks.

Ritual is a theme of Warren Lehrer, whose artists books explore the theater of life and relationships between individuals and social structures.

Power is a theme of the Guerrilla Girls, whose work seeks to overcome the marginalization of sexism and male privilege.

Much contemporary design work originates in addressing social issues, whether individual or collective, public or private.

Four common and overarching themes are identity, place, ritual, and power. Identity refers to the exploration of one's self relative to a collective identity. Place refers to the exploration of the spaces, locations, and objects that define and outline our environment. Ritual refers to the exploration of the traditions and conventions that make up our lives, such as the celebration of holidays, weddings, or simple routines (placing phone calls or doing the laundry). Power refers to the exploration of control, dominance, and privilege.

Through the filter of any of these themes, designs can be further explored in themes of consumption (use of the natural landscape and human-made goods and messages), sustainability (impact of humans on the planet), and power (ability or inability to participate and express).

Content Value

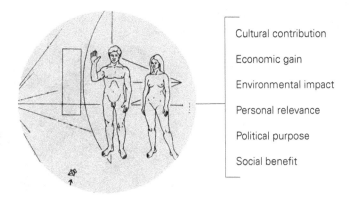

Cultural contribution

Economic gain

Environmental impact

Personal relevance

Political purpose

Social benefit

2.10
Detail of Pioneer 10
plaque

Select aspects that may determine value

On an average day, a person living in the United States is exposed to thousands of print and digital visual messages, from advertisements to traffic signs. Determining the value of these messages is an everyday and necessary occurrence, however mundane and subconscious.

A message's value, like its meaning, is open to interpretation and can be created by aspects that range from social benefit to personal relevance. Whether a message is informative, persuasive, or merely enlightening, its perceived value depends on the lens of the interpreter and the particular aspects examined.

2.11
Cave marking, 15000 BC
Lascaux, France

Pictograph

2.12
Clay tablet, 3000 BC
Damascus, Syria

Ideogram

15000 BC Pictograph

3000 BC Ideogram

1500 BC Alphabet

2.13
Evolution of communication
systems

Symbols and alphabets are codes that allow for the transmission and understanding of complex messages. They are the foundation of writing, which is a sign system that represents speech. These forms of communication have evolved over thousands of years and continue to do so in response to social, cultural, philosophical, and technological changes.

Early humans communicated through pictographs; from these came more complex pictographs and early writing systems. Some of these systems contained up to 2,000 symbols that, when combined, communicated ideas and aided recall. Ideograms evolved primarily in China at about the same time. These are symbols that stand for an idea but are not phonetic representations of spoken language. Ideograms are still in use today by an estimated one-fifth of the world's population and in numerous Eastern languages, some of which use over 40,000 characters.

2.14
Colophon, 1370
Yang Wei-Chen

Ideogram

2.15
Bible, 1457
Johannes Gutenberg

Alphabet

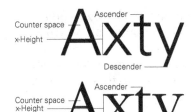

2.16
Letterform analysis
Sans-serif font (Univers), top
Serif font (Garamond), bottom

The highlighted characteristics
define legibility and personality.
Univers has a high x-Height that aids
legibility through increased white
space. The serifs of Garamond
aid readability by visually connecting
adjacent letters.

How humans transitioned from pictographs and early writing
systems to the alphabet remains unknown. The first alphabet,
named for the first two letters of the Greek alphabet,
alpha and beta, is believed to be Phoenician in origin (1500
–700BC) This alphabet eventually developed into the Roman
alphabet around the 6th century BC Alphabetic systems
use a limited number of symbols that represent individual
spoken sounds.

Technology has played a significant role in the appearance
and use of various fonts in disseminating messages. Advances
in printing in the mid-15th century in Korea and in Europe
by Johannes Gutenberg allowed for faster, less expensive
duplication of written messages.

The basic characteristics of fonts influence their use and
readability. Many designers believe that readability is a result
of repeated exposure to a font, while others believe that
certain fonts are inherently more readable.

For a closer look, see Chapter 7

2.17
Digital Synesthesia, 2005
Christy Matson

When touched, this woven piece creates sound by activating embedded copper threads connected to speakers.

> "**What matters today is locating your position, finding vantage points from which to understand the world.**"[7]
>
> Andrew Blauvelt

Public messages including billboards are governed by rules on size, placement, and illumination, along with strategies designed to target a particular audience. Public messages both influence the physical landscape in which they are viewed and contribute to and perhaps reflect the greater cultural landscape.

By contrast, private messages, such as that in a Valentine's Day card, are typically guided by cultural conventions of interaction and personal expectations. While a billboard and a personal love note certainly differ, both have targeted audiences and may seek to persuade, inform, and enlighten.

For a closer look, see Chapter 7

2.18
Potatoland (potatoland.org/riot), 2007
Mark Napier

The technology employed on this
web site allows viewers to visually
deconstruct digital messages
and to create new forms in response.

"Societies have always
been shaped more by the
nature of the media by
which men communicate
than by the content
of the communication."[8]

Marshall McLuhan and
Quentin Fiore

**Computer-mediated
communication (CMC)**
refers to computer-based
communication, including
e-mail and instant messaging.
Research suggests that, in
some situations, CMC can be
as effective as face-to-face
interaction.

Technology has a profound influence on the appearance
of visual messages and our interpretation and resulting
responses to them. Increasingly, technology offers
the possibility of audience participation through visual
and audible interfaces that allow users and viewers to
edit and select content. This changes our role as audience
and our sense of place and identity; information access
is no longer strictly controlled by physical location.

Some 600 years ago, the invention of the printing press
profoundly changed the relationship between those who
held power and those who did not by allowing information
to be duplicated and thus widely distributed. In the
digital age, information is now virtually instantaneous
and can be retrieved and archived easily.

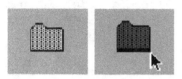

2.19
Digital interface
signals

2.20
Door handle

The use and meaning of forms can be clarified or clouded by accompanying messages. The word *push* on this door seems to contradict the design of the handle.

"A sucessful interface is like a doorknob. Users subconsciously turn it to enter and exit a room without thinking of it as the interface to the room"[9]

Donald Norman

Signals and cues are visual or auditory indicators. A signal indicates the expectation that an action will be performed, whereas a cue indicates that an action has been completed.

We live in a world of signals and cues, the visual and auditory indicators that we receive and interpret throughout the day and transmit ourselves, whether through clothing, physical gestures, or speech.

Common inanimate objects, from vending machines to ATMs, also send signals and cues. Blinking lights, sounds, or text displays help users know what to do and when they have done something correctly.

From viewing imagery and reading text in routine situations to interacting in unfamiliar environments, our ability to understand signals and cues is important in making an experience valuable.

2.21
Manual for Apparition Recorder,
2006
Heejin Kim

2.22
Gas, 1940
Edward Hopper

Kim appropriates the visual language and text from a
tape recorder instruction manual to explore role and
relationship issues (readers are expected to follow proven
procedures to happiness). Hopper explores the solitude
and longing of life in contemplative scenes.

Narratives are stories told by
a narrator. Unlike a news account,
in which groups of facts or
observations are reported, a
narrative is an interwoven
collection of memories, facts,
and observations. The word
narrative originates from
the Latin *narrare*, to recount.

Storytelling is an ancient and enduring art used to
recount events, teach, explain, and entertain. Whether
conveyed visually or orally, a story needs compelling
characters and a sense of pacing that builds drama and
balances anticipation and tension with visually or audibly
quiet moments. Interactions of images, shapes, or
colors can imply a storyline.

Narratives are a form of storytelling that involve the
interaction of characters over a set period of time.
Traditionally, narratives have a beginning, when
introductions are made; a middle, when the characters
and plot are developed, and an end, when events come
together and conclusions are drawn.

Narratives can be told from a single perspective or point
of view or from multiple and competing perspectives.
In digital form, readers can assume the role of editors as
they are given control over the story's outcome.

27

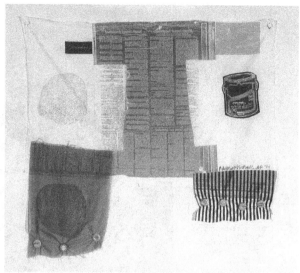

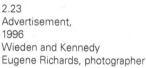

2.23
Advertisement,
1996
Wieden and Kennedy
Eugene Richards, photographer

2.24
Airport:
Cat Paws, 1974
Robert
Rauschenberg

Advertising often appropriates commonly held perceptions, such as the cowboy as rugged and adventuresome. Rauschenberg uses overt and obscure signifiers–elements that create, or point to, "coded" meanings. When the signifiers are "decoded," they reveal additional meanings.

Appropriation is the adoption of cultural imagery, conventions, visual languages, or traditions for use often unrelated to the original context. Commentary and persuasion are two common motives.

Coding and decoding refer to the act of putting together and analytically taking apart a message. Codes can be visual signifiers that, when decoded, yield new understanding.

Denotation and connotation relate to the meaning of objects. Denotation refers to the physical appearance of an object: a square is a shape with four equal sides. Connotation refers to an interpretation of an object: a square can suggest neutrality or stability.

Representation describes a human-constructed image, whether through images, typography, or symbols. In the broadest sense, representations are in all two-dimensional forms, from photographs and paintings to traffic signs.

Symbolism uses images or elements as "codes" to express intangible, complex, or multiple meanings. Coded symbols are learned or understood through the act of decoding, which is an analysis of the context, purpose, and audience of a message.

An image can be interpreted in three basic ways: literal (what we see); textural (where it fits into a story or text); and intertextual (how it references other images, styles, or events).

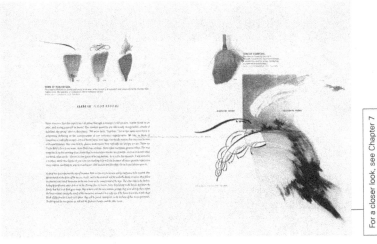

For a closer look, see Chapter 7

2.25
Calla Leaves, 1929
Imogen Cunningham

2.26
Visible Citizens, 2002
Stephen Farrell, co-author and designer; Steve Tomasula, co-author; and Jiwon Son, designer

Cunningham used natural forms as a metaphor for sensual growth and discovery. Farrell used common household objects as analogies to support a story of personal discovery.

Metaphors are the use of a word or image to suggest comparison to another object or concept.

A metaphor is a vehicle for revealing a deeper meaning and understanding of complex or abstract concepts. Like representation, metaphors are found in all visual forms of two-dimensional design because they represent ideas, concerns, or physical objects.

Aristotle said that a good metaphor implies an intuitive perception of the similarity between dissimilar things. Some shapes or colors can assume meaning beyond their primary or literal appearance. Whether abstract or literal, the elements carry references to other events or meanings that can enrich the overall message.

Analogy is another form of symbolism and is related to metaphor. But whereas a metaphorical object alone can represent and, in a sense, replace a concept, an analogical object is simply added to other images or text and helps support or contribute to the concept.

Applying Theories and Methodologies Introduction to Two-Dimensional Design

Applying Theories and Methodologies

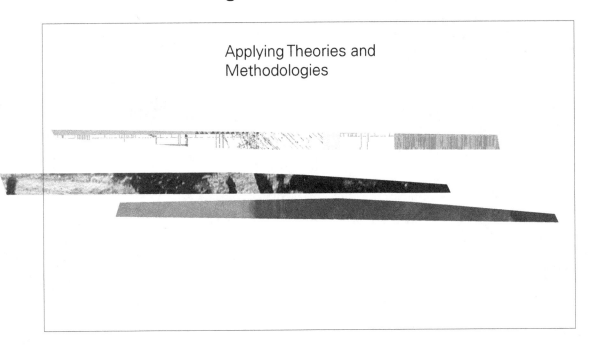

Concepts

Theory
Gestalt
Semiotics
Information Organization

Methodologies
Types
Function
Collaboration
Intuition
Research
Strategy

Problem Solving
Function
Process
Components

This chapter examines how methodologies
of creating, targeting, and disseminating visual
messages play a role in shaping interpretation
and response.

Applying Theories and Methodologies

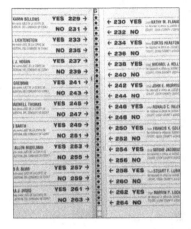

3.1
Ballot design, 2000
Designer unknown

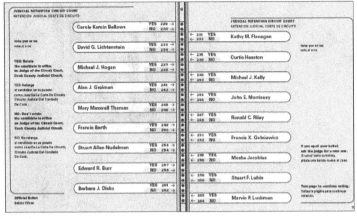

3.2
Ballot redesign, 2004
Design for Democracy

More accurate positioning of candidates to their respective punch holes has greatly reduced voter error.

"You have to doubt all the time, [you have to] feel unsatisfied until, for some reason, and that is the mystery of the design process, until you feel it [the solution] is the one that is right."[10]

Mario Bellini

Contemporary design work is influenced by theories from a range of disciplines. These theories are, in turn, organized and applied through methodologies that guide explorations.

Some two-dimensional design work incorporates quantitative methods – clearly defined and observable – akin to those used in the sciences. Other design work may rely more on qualitative methods – subjective, perhaps not repeatable – such as intuition, experience, simple common sense, or sudden inspiration. Design as an activity is similar to many disciplines in the humanities in that different methods can be chosen to solve the same problem and result in very different, yet appropriate solutions.

3.3
Cover for
The Dada Painters, 1951
Paul Rand

This work exhibits four primary aspects of gestalt: closure, continuance, proximity, and similarity.

3.4
The Kitchen Knife Cuts through the Weimar Beer-Belly Culture, 1919
Hannah Hoch

A montage from the Dada movement, whose members explored methods of chance and visual play in creating social messages.

Led by Swiss psychologist Max Wertheimer, Gestalt psychology began in Europe in the early 1900s. This branch of psychology examines how we perceive visual form by organizing its components into a meaningful whole.

Gestalt's basic premise is that organization is central to all mental activity and reflects how our brains function. Using Gestalt, the whole is understood to be different from the sum of its parts. Translated from German, Gestalt means "entire figure or configuration."

Gestalt theory was later popularized by Rudolf Arnheim, an American psychologist and philosopher who was one of the first to apply its principles to the study of art. A form that exhibits high organization has "good" gestalt, where *good* means simple or regular and is not a value judgment, while a form with low organization has "weak" gestalt.

  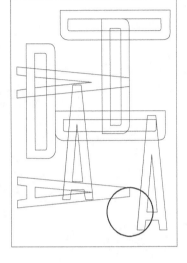

3.5
Closure

The grouping's external
boundary creates a
unified shape.

3.6
Continuance

Letters remain
readable despite
overlapping.

3.7
Proximity and similarity

Letters share
common
characteristics.

**"Visual form must also
be considered as a basic
means of understanding
the environment.
Man's notions of what
things are, how they act,
and how they are related
to each other rely greatly
on appearance."**[11]

Rudolf Arnheim

Gestalt's four aspects are closure, continuance, proximity,
and similarity. Individually or collectively, these aspects
help us understand form as a meaningful whole and not as
isolated, unrelated parts.

Closure occurs when a form's separate elements create a
unified grouping rather than clusters of disparate parts.

Continuance occurs when part of a form overlaps itself or
an adjacent part without interrupting our ability to understand
each part as a whole.

Proximity refers to the distance between parts comprising
a form. Elements that are closer together appear to be related.

Similarity among parts in a form helps hold the form
together. Elements that are similar appear related.

Theory Semiotics

3.8
U.S. Department
of Transportation sign

Official signage is the result of extensive
audience testing and relies on established
theories including semiotics.

Semiotic theory was first outlined in the 1930s by American
philosopher Charles Morris, who believed that an analysis
of visual and verbal signs could lead toward more effective
communication. In this context, the term *sign* means a
visual concept, not literally a sign. A photograph, painting,
or symbol might contain many signs that the viewer puts
together to create a whole and derive meaning.

As a branch of linguistics, semiotic theory has become a
useful tool in applied design when creating and evaluating
messages seen by diverse audiences. Semiotics is divided
into three areas: syntactic, which is the examination of
organization and relationships; semantic, the examination of
significance and purpose; and pragmatic, the examination
of application and effects.

3.9
Pedestrian crossing sign

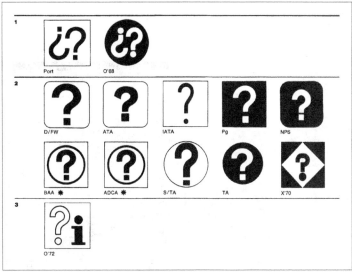

3.10
Global informational sign
study, 1993

Symbols from around the world that express
common functions to varied audiences
were collected and evaluated according to the
three aspects of semiotic theory.

Representation is created
through the use of *symbols*, in
which a sign's meaning is
culturally agreed upon, such as
the letters XING to abbreviate
the word crossing; *icons*, in
which a sign's meaning is derived
from resemblance to an object,
such as the walking pedestrian
depicted on a pedestrian
crossing sign; and *indexes*, in
which a sign's meaning is
derived through reasoning and
association, such as two parallel
lines surrounding a pedestrian
icon to indicate a crosswalk and
safety zone.

When used together, the three aspects of semiotic theory
can aid in the design and evaluation of visual messages.

Syntactic refers to the formal relationship among elements
in a form or among related forms. When analyzing a form
for its syntactic qualities, an important question is: Are all
parts of the form arranged to appear unified?

Semantic refers to the relationship between a form and
its meaning. When analyzing a form for semantic qualities,
typical questions are: Does the form adequately reflect
its meaning? Is the meaning singular or multiple, ambiguous
or clear? Which of these is more desirable?

Pragmatic refers to the relationship between a form and
its user. This aspect examines a sign when it is applied.
When analyzing a form for its pragmatic qualities, consider
these questions: Is the form related to its context? Is it
understandable in its context?

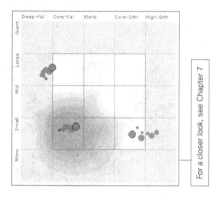

3.11
San Francisco Guide, 2006
Chuck Byrne

Continuum and location

3.12
Pacific Bell White Pages, 1997
Matthew Carter, Font Designer

Alphabetical

3.13
Morningstar Mutual Fund Report, 2007
Philip Burton

Category and time

As the human population grows and technology development accelerates, the amount of information we receive increases exponentially. We receive much of the information visually, through print and digital media. We also receive information through exchange with others, through listening to our bodies (such as feeling hot or cold as a signal of being sick), and through everyday observation and participation in the human-made and natural environment.

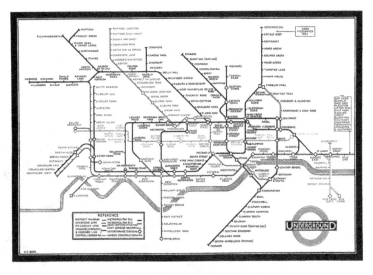

3.14
London Underground map, 1933
Henry Beck

Location

Considered a hallmark in the field of information design, this work brings clarity to a highly complex network through the use of simple and repeated graphic elements, angles, and typographic positioning.

Alphabetical Listing
North America
South America

Alphabetical/Numerical Listing
1 North America
2 South America

3.15
Common listing methods

The way information is presented can suggest a value judgment.

Methods of organizing information can be used exclusively or in combination.

Alphabetical refers to organization based on the order of the letters of the alphabet.

Category refers to organization based on types or models, such as a grocery list or receipt.

Continuum refers to organization based on comparisons between or among elements, such as color or shape.

Location refers to organization that identifies the position of objects.

Time refers to organization based on the time or date of an event.

Methodologies Types

3.16
HMS Montezuma, 1942

Camouflage is the result of research in visual perception. The camouflage on this World War II British warship is intended to alter the ship's perceived speed, size, class, type, and model.

Methodology is a select grouping of concepts, ideas, processes, or theories used to guide an investigation and its underlying assumptions. Method refers to specific processes or sequences of events used by a methodology.

Methodologies guide research by providing a structure for accomplishing something in a meaningful way. Methodologies can be structured, rational, and deliberate, progressing linearly through clearly articulated and repeatable procedures, or they can be loosely defined, intuitive, and subconsciously applied.

Most methodologies used in two-dimensional design are categorized as "problem solving." Problem solving is generally linear and deductive, beginning with a broad view and narrowing down to a specific solution based on reasoning drawn from and dependent on the method used.

3.17
IDEO method cards, 2004
IDEO

Divided into four conceptual categories—learn, look, ask, and try—
these cards help the studio's clients establish strategic goals through
browsing, grouping, and discussing visual form and concepts.

Process refers to a sequence
of events that culminate in
a result. Processes occur
throughout nature and in human
activity, such as in the process
of learning. Many processes
are recurring and repeatable,
although the results may differ.

Methodologies can aid in understanding and interpreting
bodies of knowledge, social and cultural phenomena, and the
relationships among parts of a whole.

3.18
Do It Yourself Exhibition, 2006
Ellen Lupton, Curator

As active participants in this exhibition, the audience collected, edited, and posted printed material from public and private spaces.

Collaboration is a process between two or more people who work together to achieve common goals.

"To really be successful you need to get a lot of people involved." 12

Linus Torvalds

Work that seeks to reveal complex relationships, express deep social issues, or employ new methods often benefits from collaboration.

Collaboration is a powerful tool for the exchange of ideas. The opinions and experiences of others can expand possibilities and bring new and unexpected results.

Collaboration can take many forms, from designers working together on a team to direct audience participation during the creation or evaluation stage of a work. Effective collaboration requires good listening skills, cooperation, and fair decision making.

3.19
Jackson Pollock
East Hampton Studio, 1943
Hans Namuth, photographer

Jackson Pollock's work is known for its materials and format (paint dripped onto flat canvas) and his intuitive, emotional responses to their visual qualities.

Intuition refers to decision making based on instinct or innate knowledge.

As a creative act, design has aspects that elude concise explanation and description. Design decisions can spring from a moment, the influence of a person or place, or an individual's "gut feeling."

Honed by experience and feeling, intuition is a form of common sense and a guiding force throughout all of life. While shaped by outside forces, such as politics, economics, or spiritual experiences, intuition can't be taught; it can only be applied and experienced.

Design methods and processes typically include some rational, analytical, methodical, and often repeatable components. But decisions based on intuition are ever-present throughout everyone's design process.

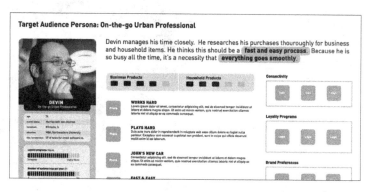

Target Audience Persona: On-the-go Urban Professional

Devin manages his time closely. He researches his purchases thouroughly for business and household items. He thinks this should be a **fast and easy process**. Because he is so busy all the time, it's a necessity that **everything goes smoothly.**

DEVIN
On-the-go Urban Professional

3.20
Audience persona, 2007
John DeVylder

Audience personas are commonly used in applied design to help position a product to the targeted market. Personas summarize the habits, desires, and needs of a fictional person based on market research.

Maslow's Hierarchy of Needs are self-actualization (creativity), esteem (respect and achieve-ment), love (belonging and intimacy), safety (income and relationships), and physiological (food and shelter) — all strategic marketing targets.

Self-Actualization
Esteem
Love
Safety
Physiological

3.21
Maslow's Hierarchy of Needs

Research helps us understand and interpret our natural and human-made environment. Its general purpose is to create new information, clarify relationships or bodies of accepted knowledge, or critically interpret existing information.

Applied design activity such as graphic design (which generally has a specific audience and seeks a specific response) can employ the research methods or results from other disciplines. Such activity is influenced by ethnographic research in the discipline of anthropology as well as psychology and sociology.

Design research often takes the form of interviews among designers and clients, focus group tests of the target audience, written audience interaction scenarios, or collection of visual materials from peers. Through these, information is analyzed and used to create concepts that more effectively target audiences.

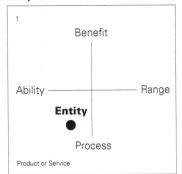

Entity Now

Benefit

Ability —————— Range

Entity

Process

Product or Service

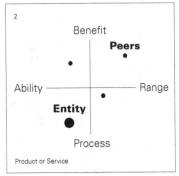

Entity and Peers Now

Benefit

Peers

Ability —————— Range

Entity

Process

Product or Service

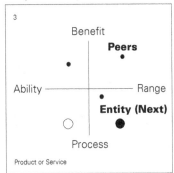

Entity Next **and Peers** Next?

Benefit

Peers

Ability —————— Range

Entity (Next)

Process

Product or Service

3.22
Positioning matrix

A matrix can help guide or define an entity's marketing strategies. Multiple matrices can be used to visualize aspects such as the target audience, institutional mission, and long-term goals.

Strategy is a plan of action designed to achieve a particular goal or goals. Effective strategies attempt to anticipate changing conditions such as user traits or to redefine existing relationships among audiences, products, and messages.

"Design is a potent strategy tool that companies can use to gain a competitive advantage." [13]

Philip Kotler

Few of the visual forms and messages we encounter are the product of chance. During a city commute, for example, the traffic signs, the frequency of the billboards, and even the placement of graffiti are all planned interactions.

Strategies are developed with thorough knowledge of the situation: the entity (what is its purpose?), the product or service (what is the objective?), the history (what has been done before?), the target audience (to whom is the work directed?), and the competition (what else is being done and how?). Information gathered through research can be visualized and analyzed through positioning matrices. These in turn can direct the creation of visuals possessing attributes that support strategic positioning goals.

Problem Solving Function

Abilities of the audience

Regulatory/social constraints

Possibilities of the media

Social/environmental implications

Strategic goals

Viewing/using context

3.23
Problem-solving
overview

Problem solving can aid in the identification, organization, and prioritization of a project's components.

Problem solving has four basic components: learning, identifying, generating, and implementing. It is most effective when the process facilitates researching as well as solving by expanding a problem's posed conditions, such as constraints or preconceived outcomes.

A specific design activity or project can be referred to as a problem or series of problems. The word problem in this context signifies a challenge, an opportunity to create a meaningful outcome.

The act of problem solving involves identifying a problem or set of conditions, then arriving at an outcome in a consistent and enlightened manner. The problem is approached critically and deliberately rather than casually or passively. While a critical approach doesn't necessarily rule out chance or sudden inspiration, it does offer the opportunity to direct it.

When broadly applied, problem solving underlies all of life's activities. It can be used to create a form, a method of organization, or a course of action.

Problem Solving Process

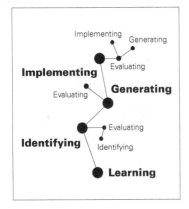
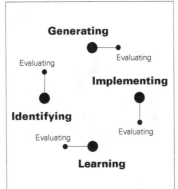
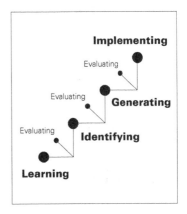

3.24
Problem-solving process

Psychologists have identified four primary approaches to problem solving: linear, branching, circular, and a combination of the two.

Divergent and convergent thinking refers to thinking broadly (divergent) to create multiple options and then focusing (convergent) on select concepts based on deductive reasoning and formed conclusions. Problem-solving explorations move from the divergent to the convergent throughout the creative process; the interplay between the two generates and refines options.

Every person's problem-solving process is unique, but in general most processes fall into the basic components of learning, identifying, generating, and implementing. While the first three components are typically divergent and the last component convergent, explorations can move from divergent to convergent at any point.

Applying Theories and Methodologies   Introduction to Two-Dimensional Design

Learning Understanding a Problem

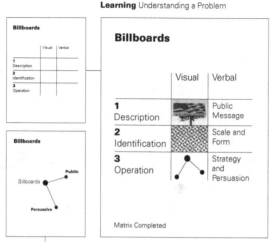

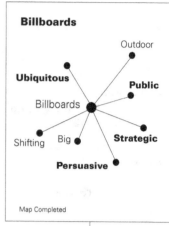

A visualization matrix and thinking map started (above) and completed (right).

3.25
Visualization
Matrix

3.26
Thinking
Map

Visualization matrices use images and words as an aid to understanding and creating visuals. Common categories include description (what is it?), identification (what defines it?), and operation (how does it work?).

Thinking maps are based on related descriptive words chosen by free association and placed in an expanding fashion to further understanding of the center word.

Learning conditions and becoming familiar with all aspects of the situation are typically the first steps. Focus can be directed to the work's audience and to the physical environment in which the work will exist. Depending on the problem at hand and whether the work is applied or non-applied, the learning process might involve conducting ethnographic studies of how people interact with objects or messages, conducting client interviews, performing visual audits (collection and analysis of peer material), or researching a particular social issue or physical location.

Identifying and defining the problem follows. Information gathered in the previous step is analyzed. From this, a strategic plan is typically developed, the main issues are identified, and a plan is developed that considers all reasonable options and their implications. Concepts that drive visual decision making are often created at this point.

Problem Solving Components

Identifying Developing concepts

Generating Giving form to concepts

Implementing Choosing and refining forms

Questions

How can the viewer of a billboard become more active?

When can a composition illuminate underlying billboard strategies and agendas?

Attributes

Confused	Revealing
Connected	Shifting
Exposed	Temporary
Juxtaposed	Unfinished
Layered	Vulnerable

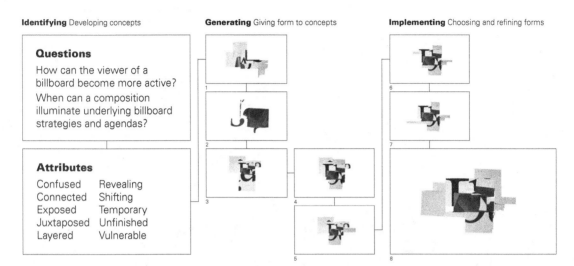

3.27
Process example, 2007
John Bowers

This work, composed of discarded billboards, employs basic problem-solving components: learning (analysis of the billboard's verbal and visual languages), identifying (development and visualization of concepts), generating (creation of small studies using billboard pieces), and implementing (refinement and enlargement of studies into final works).

Attribute lists are a collection of adjectives that describe a work's visual expression. Created early in the problem-solving process, they can direct all visual decision making, including the choice of color palettes or fonts.

Generating ideas and selecting solutions further the process. Possible solutions can take the form of visually loose hand sketches or computer-developed iterations. Often a concept, or parts of a concept, becomes useful later as the project is further defined. From these loose iterations or "directions," one or more can be chosen and refined.

Implementing solutions and evaluating results is the final step, when an outcome is applied and evaluated. Depending on the original problem, a solution's value can be determined through usability testing (common in web site design), informal exchange with the audience, or peer review.

Exploring
Visual Components

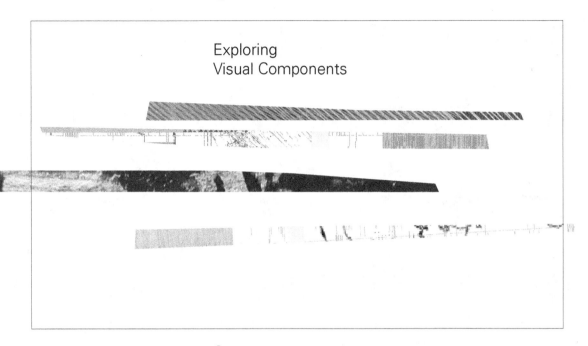

Concepts

Presentations
Literal
Abstract
Symbolic

Form
Geometric
Organic

Elements
Dot and Line
Plane and Volume

Characteristics
Size and Scale
Shape and Texture

Principles
Position and Direction

Interactions
Space
Negative Space
Depth and Perspective
Visual Weight and Balance
Asymmetry and Symmetry

This chapter identifies and analyzes the basic components of visual form.

Exploring Visual Components

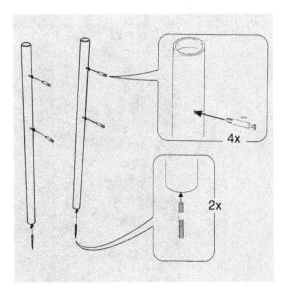

4.1
Instructions for furniture
assembly, 1995
IKEA

Basic elements such as lines can be
used to group and separate information
and direct action.

All visual form is composed of three components:
elements, characteristics, and interactions. Visual elements
are dots, lines, planes, and volumes; each element
possesses characteristics of size, shape, texture, and
color. These elements and characteristics are directed by
principles of visual interaction, which include position,
direction, and space.

Although components can be individually identified and
studied, they influence or are influenced by other
components in the form. We can therefore best evaluate
components by comparing them to other components
and by observing our position relative to them. For example,
we can determine an object's size by comparing it to
another object and our distance from it.

Presentations Overview

4.2
Identity Image, 1997
Johnson and Wolverton

Forms can use a combination of presentations simultaneously. This work uses overlapping low-resolution imagery that, in places, is literal, abstract, and symbolic.

Basic visual components can be used to create literal, abstract, or symbolic form. These presentations take different approaches in conveying ideas and concepts, and serve different purposes.

The appropriateness of a presentation depends primarily on the subject to be depicted and the purpose and context of the message. Philosophical movements and cultural trends can also influence the use of one presentation over another.

Abstraction, for example, became a dominant means of presentation in the early 20th century. Its emergence was based on discoveries and thinking that questioned accepted beliefs across many disciplines, including the absolute nature of time in work that conveys relativity by simultaneously presenting multiple views of a single object. By departing from literal presentation, abstraction extended the ability to represent this new thinking.

4.3
Illustrated page, 1890
Artist unknown

Literal

4.4
Untitled Study, 1962
Patrick Bowers

Abstract

4.5
Stanzas from "The Crab Canon," 1747
Johann Sebastian Bach

Symbolic

Literal presentation depicts an object or concept through detailed realism without unnecessary embellishment and exaggeration. It can be based on close observation of an object and provide a record of subtleties in a complex form.

Abstract presentation, by contrast, is deliberate simplification, often with exaggeration. This method can be based on close observation of an object or can explore the relationships among various forms alone, without direct observation. It is particularly useful for depicting difficult concepts, ideas, or thoughts because it excludes unimportant areas and focuses on areas critical to meaning.

Symbolic presentation uses symbols to convey complex technical information or highly abstract concepts that must be made clear to others. The symbols are generally not based on an object but are arbitrarily designed, with their meaning assigned and agreed upon, and learned by the audience.

Form Geometric

4.6
Interior based on tatami

Tatami straw floor mats have been used for centuries in Japanese homes, where tatami proportions (a rectangle of two squares) also dictate the size and shape of the rooms.

4.7
Common geometric shapes and applications

Literal, abstract, and symbolic presentations can result in geometric or organic form, or a combination of the two.

Geometric form has regular angles or patterns and is commonly made up of circles, triangles, squares, or combinations of these. It is found in nature, such as in the crystalline structures of rocks or snowflakes, and applied in human-made form when easy recognition is required, such as for a stop sign.

Form Organic

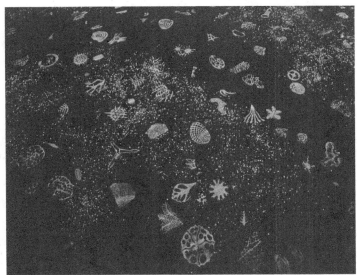

4.8
Inspiration for *A Walk on the Beach*

4.9
A Walk on the Beach,
1995
Michele Oka Doner
Miami International Airport

Saltwater plants and shells from Florida beaches were the inspiration for this work. Two thousand flat, bronze-cast elements were embedded in the concourse floor to reflect the movement of the water toward and away from the shore.

4.10
Organic shapes
from *A Walk on the Beach*

Organic form can have a fluid appearance. Nature offers an abundant supply of organic shapes, patterns, and complex structures, including shells, leaves, and petals, and the fluid, natural movements of waves and tides. Such organic forms have long served as inspiration for artists and designers.

Elements Dot and Line

Close uses dots as the building components of identifiable form. While the form can be viewed as a whole, it also conveys a sense of fragmentation.

4.11
Self Portrait,
1977
Chuck Close

4.12
The Marketplace,
1930
Diego Rivera

A highly expressive example of simple outline (contour) lines.

4.13
Dot

4.14
Line

Whether geometric or organic, all form is built on the basic elements of dots, lines, planes, and volumes. These elements alone can connote strong emotional qualities.

Dots are the visual expression of a point, which is an indicator of location. A dot can take any simple shape, whether geometric or organic.

Lines are the connection of two or more dots. A line can be a continuous mark, a series of short dashes, or separate dots visually connected by their similarity and placement. It can be straight or move in different directions. A line can also be a grouping of type, symbols, images, or simple markings.

Lines can create shapes and divide space. They are useful for isolating and grouping forms and information.

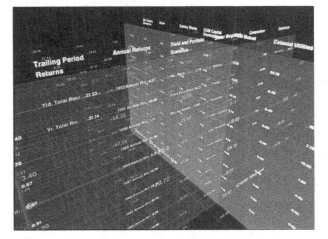

4.15
Correspondence form, 1994
Helene Jonson

4.16
Motion study, 1994
Lisa Strausfeld
(MIT Media Lab)

The thoughtful use of lines can clarify information and create an engaging visual experience. Volume is created through intersecting geometric planes that emphasize content as they move.

4.17
Plane

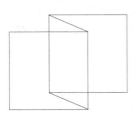

4.18
Volume

Plane refers to an area outlined by lines or defined by a grouping of images, type, symbols, or markings. It is an expression of height or length and width. The physical surface of a composition is often called the picture plane.

Volume is the product of dots, lines, and planes. It refers to the illusion of a three-dimensional form on a two-dimensional surface, and to the illusion of space within a form.

4.19
Poster for steamship line,
1931
A.M. Cassandre

4.20
Pathé Symbol, 1999
Eric Scott and Margaret
Youngblood, design directors
Landor

Dramatic size differences
between elements and the angle
of elements can create a sense
of awe and power.

4.21
Scale
Small and large

Scale refers to the relative size
relationship among objects.

Whether literal, abstract, or symbolic, geometric or
organic, all two-dimensional form shares the basic visual
characteristics of size, shape, texture, and color. (Color
has many unique characteristics and is discussed in its
own chapter.)

Size is understood in relation to other objects or to the
environment in which an element is placed. We can also
determine the size of a form by measuring its length
or height. We often make such comparisons in reference
to familiar forms or to our own height or width.

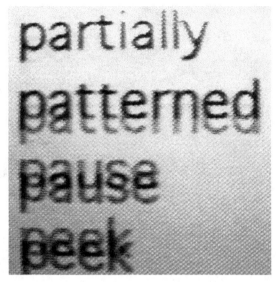

4.22
Nike symbol, 1972
Carolyn Davidson

4.23
Alphabetically Sorted, 1996
Rebeca Bollinger

A shape alone, such as that used by Nike, can serve as an identifier through repeated exposure and learned association. The above work uses texture as a device to explore the vocabulary of interactive online services.

Shape refers to the external outline (or contour) of a form.

Texture in two-dimensional form is visual and generally not tactile. It imitates tactile qualities such as rough or coarse, smooth or fine.

4.24
Common textures:

directional (top left)
non-directional (top right)
static (bottom left)
dynamic (bottom right)

4.25
Cropping and juxtaposition

4.26
Poster for the Rural
Electrification
Administration, 1937
Lester Beall

Position and direction can reinforce the
relationship of a form's elements. The background
stripes imply a flag and echo the lines of the
fence to create a direct and cohesive statement
of stability, strength, and national pride.

Cropping refers to the way an
element that appears to extend
beyond the compositional
boundaries is cut off at the
frame edge.

Juxaposition refers to the
positioning of contrasting
elements such as hard and soft,
and contrasting concepts such
as weak and strong.

Visual elements interact through position and direction.
Taken together or separately, these principles govern
the interaction of elements within a frame, which marks
the limits of a composition.

Position refers to the placement of an element relative
to other elements or to the frame.

The distance between elements and between elements
and the frame can create points of focus and tension.
If an element is positioned close to the frame edge or to
another element, the relationship between the two can
be heightened. The element can appear in its entirety or be
cropped to create a sense of movement and suggest that
the compositional area extends beyond the frame.

Direction infers a course of movement. Elements placed
in parallel directions convey similarity, while opposing
directions can suggest confrontation.

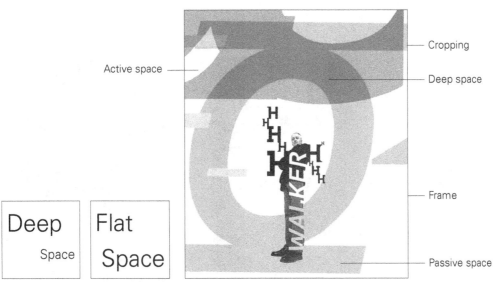

Active space

Cropping

Deep space

Frame

Passive space

4.28
Publication for the
Walker Art Center, 1998
Matt Eller

Active and passive spaces created by juxtaposed
and cropped letterforms combine to create
movement and contrasting areas of visual rest
and activity.

Deep
Space

Flat
Space

4.27
Deep space and flat space

4.29
IBM rebus, 1980, and
IBM symbol, 1956
Paul Rand

This visual pun substitutes
pictures for the first two letters
of the IBM logo. Its visual
effectiveness is achieved in
part through flat space, which
unifies the elements and
equalizes their dominance.

Space refers to the areas in, around, and between elements.
These areas can be active participants in the composition
and as dominant and important as the elements themselves.
Space can group, separate, and emphasize elements and
allow the viewer to better distinguish the elements and their
roles in a composition.

Space can be active or passive depending on the shape of
the space. Active space tends to have an irregular or complex
shape. Active space is commonly created by using overlap
or transparency. Passive space tends to have a simple shape,
with an outline composed of few directional changes.

Even the most active compositions tend to have passive
areas that provide a visual rest and that contrast with the
active areas.

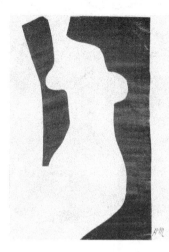

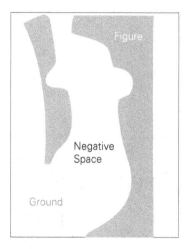

4.30
Venus, 1952
Henri Matisse

Space can
become active
and emotive
through its shape.

4.31
Negative space

4.32
World Wildlife Fund panda,
1961
Sir Peter Scott

In this work, a cohesive
symbol is created through the
use of negative space and
characteristics evoking
innocence and vulnerability.

Negative space refers to a seemingly empty but active
area of a composition. A negative area can appear to
come forward and be slightly lighter or brighter than the
surrounding elements.

Figure and ground are used to describe a perception of
spatial interaction. Figure refers to an element on the picture
plane, while ground is the larger area surrounding it.

Psychologists have studied the figure-ground relationship
and have found that we understand form if it is
distinguishable from the background. This is generally
accomplished through a difference in value (light and dark)
between the figure and the ground.

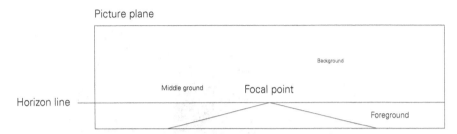

Picture plane

Horizon line

Background

Middle ground   Focal point

Foreground

Picture
Plane

4.33
Picture plane
front view (left) and
side view (right)

4.34
The Ideal City,
15th century
Piero della Francesca

Lines diverging from a single point create a
strong sense of depth, perspective, and order in
the picture plane, positioning the viewer in front
of the scene.

Depth in three-dimensional design is physically present.
In two-dimensional design, however, an illusion of
depth must be created through pictorial cues. Pictorial
cues are visual representations that signal differences or
direct understanding, and include color changes, scale,
overlap, and perspective.

Perspective on a flat, two-dimensional surface is created
through the use of lines. In linear perspective, which
is the most common method, objects are foreshortened
to give the illusion that they recede in space toward
a common point. Foreshortening is a distinctly Western
invention, refined during the Renaissance as an aid
in organizing compositional space and in lending order
to our relationship to the environment.

Light

Heavy

Heavy

Light

4.35
Visual weight

4.36
Cartography, 1996
Sam Gilliam

This composition is divided into simple units that balance one another through size, shape, position, and color. The large light spaces are balanced by the smaller, darker spaces.

Visual weight is the sum of a forms components and is akin to mass and energy. However, it cannot be touched or physically measured and thus not easily quantified. In addition, our perception of visual weight is influenced by a range of variables, including size and color.

Visual balance refers to the degree of equilibrium in a composition. This is determined by the arrangement of elements in relation to each other and to the frame. Position is the dominant means of creating balance, resulting in symmetry, asymmetry, or combinations of both.

Asymmetry refers to a form that, when split, has two halves of unequal size or shape. Also called dynamic tension or dynamic equilibrium, asymmetry is based on juxtaposition. Asymmetric balance can create an active form, compelling our eyes to move around the composition.

A sym metry	Sym metr y

4.37
Asymmetry and symmetry

4.38
Poster for library campaign, 1992
Lucille Tenazas

Asymmetry

4.39
Pages from "On doing nothing," 1992
P. Scott Makela

Symmetry

Asymmetry was used extensively in the West for much of the 20th century, in part as a rejection of established social and political structures and the symmetrical forms that communicated them. Contemporary design, in turn, has expanded the visual vocabulary and exhibits both asymmetrical and symmetrical forms of balance.

Symmetry refers to a form that can be split diagonally, vertically, or horizontally, resulting in two essentially equal halves. Bilateral symmetry (two exactly equal halves) is the most common type of symmetry. Symmetrical balance tends to create a stable form, keeping our eyes in one general location.

Symmetry is abundant in nature and is the oldest method of seeking visual balance. The Egyptians, Greeks, and Romans used symmetry to find and reveal order not only in the visual realm, but also in religion and philosophy.

5

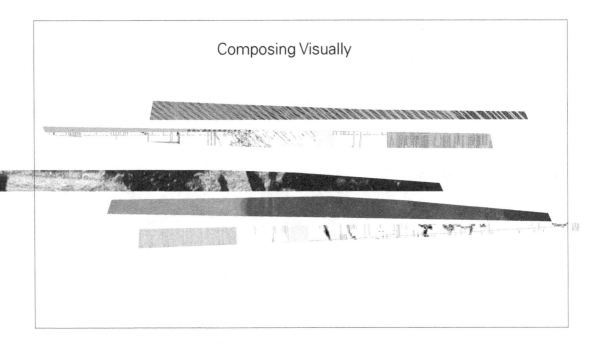

Composing Visually

Concepts

Approaches
Visual Language
Theme and Variation

Principles
Continuity
Contrast
Hierarchy
Emphasis
Rhythm
Time and Sequencing

Methods
Structure
Grids
Proportions
Geometry
Golden Section
Root 2

This chapter examines how compositions can be approached and visual components can be applied to create a range of visual forms and messages.

Composing Visually

5.1
Amish split-bars quilt,
Lancaster County, Pennsylvania, 1900
Designer unknown

"Form Follows Function." [15]

Horatio Greenough

Composition refers to the arrangement of visual elements and their characteristics within a defined area. Visual composition is similar to composition in other activities, such as writing and music, in which a sense of unity is sought. While unity can involve some degree of discord or tension that attracts us, it is balanced by an overall cohesiveness. A form that balances change with a level of consistency among its parts is often visually engaging.

A form's composition can emphasize parts of information, reveal relationships among components, and guide interpretation. This can be done by making some aspects more dominant than others to create different levels of attention. Structure can also be used to create order and unity in a single composition or across several forms that are seen together as a group.

71

5.2
Convenience store signage
and British Petroleum (BP) symbol

Vernacular/corporate

5.3
U.S. Department of Transportation
signage and guerrilla sticker

Official/unofficial

Visual language can express
dualities between official and unofficial
design roles and vernacular and
corporate communication types.

Visual language is a mode
of expression. It is a combination
of style, visual elements,
and media.

Vernacular design is
work done by those without
formal design training that
often expresses regional styles
and is made with inexpensive
materials.

"Less is more" [16]

Ludwig Mies van der Rohe
1947

"Less is a bore" [17]

Robert Venturi
1966

In the broadest sense, a visual language is a system of
elements arranged according to the principles of a particular
activity, entity, or movement. It is a reflection of taste and
style but chosen and applied by strategies and agendas —
determining factors in appearance and usage. Visual
languages are perhaps best described through dualities
such as official and unofficial, corporate and vernacular.
In contemporary design, a broad range of languages
are employed simultaneously by different entities to address
similar issues or problems.

For a closer look, see Chapter 7

5.4
*The Wood Letters
of the Greenwood Press*, 1975
Jack Stauffacher

Stauffacher extends the function
of simple letters through playful and
generative visual clusters.

Generative work builds
upon itself and expands in
the process. It is a less linear
or methodical form of
theme and variation in that
all aspects of the process
are led by the preceding result
but open to incremental or
drastic change.

Theme and variation are a common form of divergent and
convergent thinking used to generate a work. A theme
might be a concept, a way of working, an issue, or a visual
relationship.

Variation refers to the process of change through which
something is altered without losing a sense of the underlying
theme. This process can facilitate in-depth explorations
and produce thoughtful work.

An underlying structure upon
which elements are placed creates
continuity and, in this example, a
thoughtful rhythm among elements.

5.5
Pages from National Gallery
of Art Catalog *Quiet Beauty,* 2003
Antonio Alcala

5.6
*The Three
Women,* 1908
Pablo Picasso

Intersecting
planes are used
to create a sense
of unity.

Human needs are typically met through interactions
that exhibit meaningful organization rather than
chaos. Underlying design activity is the search for such
meaning through the unification of visual elements
and concepts. A unified composition can provide
viewers with a better understanding of its purpose and
a more cohesive visual presence. Such forms can also
express continuity when our eyes are led continuously
among a composition's visual elements or multiple forms
in a group.

For a closer look, see Chapter 7

5.7
Unsymmetry, 2006
Hu Hung-Shu

Hu's paintings use light and dark areas to create shifting horizontal movements.

Contrast refers to differences among elements and their degree of conflict or discord. These differences are often described in relative terms such as high contrast and low contrast.

We tend to favor compositions in which the parts are related in some way yet different, however subtle or pronounced. Contrast can attract and maintain our attention and move our eyes to specific areas. It can also help us better understand the parts that make up the whole and differentiate among types of information.

Contrast can be achieved through opposing visual elements, such as the round edge of a circle against the sharp corner of a square, a light area against a dark area, or a large element against a small element.

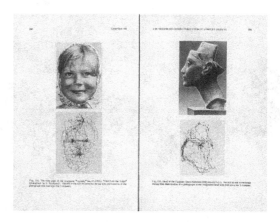

5.8
Pages from *Eye Movements and Reading Orders*, 1967
Dr. Alfred L. Yarbus

This time-lapse record of eye movement shows how we focus on the most informative and characteristic aspects of form.

Hierarchy refers to the levels of emphasis or importance in a composition. From business to sports, organized human expressions and activities that join people in reaching common goals exhibit some degree of hierarchy.

Capturing, maintaining, and focusing attention are important considerations in strengthening the appearance and meaning of a form. The choice and arrangement of components can lead our eyes in a particular direction and keep them there, or encourage them to move on. Research into how humans examine complex objects suggests that we are primarily attracted to elements in a composition we consider important and essential to understanding.

Through the use of hierarchy, attention can be drawn to certain components or ideas arranged in dominant versus subordinate areas. Hierarchy can make a composition more active and engaging and aid the viewer in discerning which elements belong together. When some elements are presented as dominant over others, it is easier to understand the whole form.

Secondary Primary   Tertiary

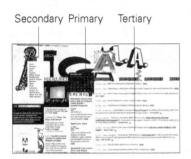

Primary Secondary Tertiary

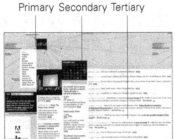

5.9
American Institute of Graphic Arts,
Los Angeles, web site, 2007
Ed Fella (left) and
David Handschuh (right)

Through the use of visual interfaces
called skins, this web site allows
users to change the hierarchy and
emphasis of content.

5.10
Emiliano Zapata,
1995
Mauricio Lasansky

A focal point
can contribute
to the character
of a work.

An emphasis or focal point in a composition can draw
attention to a specific area and direct the composition's
interpretation. Emphasis can help viewers discern
differences and determine relationships. Levels of attention
can be created though primary, secondary, and tertiary
pieces of information (common in graphic design),
and through foreground, middle, and background layers
(common in representational drawing and painting).

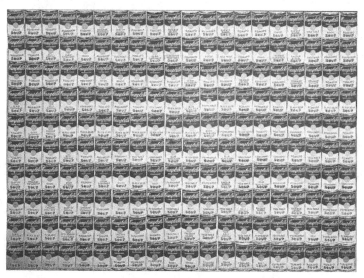

5.11
Bar code

5.12
*Two Hundred
Campbell's Soup Cans*,
1962
Andy Warhol

The spacing between the vertical lines of a bar code not only conveys pricing information, but also creates a simple visual rhythm. Through repetition, Warhol comments on mass production and the icons of popular culture.

Pattern is created through the repetition of individual elements to form a larger grouping.

The natural environment provides an abundance of physical forms, patterns, and movements that establish rhythms. Since the beginning of recorded history, nature has influenced the creation of human-made rhythms. The Nile's periodic flooding in ancient times, for example, inspired the creation of scales to mark flood levels and calendars to identify harvest times. Today, we continue to use nature's rhythms and movements — the Earth's revolution around the sun, the weather, the temperature — to regulate and plan our activities.

In two-dimensional design, rhythm is the movement from one idea, compositional area, or element to another. It is largely the result of structure and positioning. In music, rhythm is created through the manipulation of time between musical notes. In visual form, rhythm requires a keen sense of spacing and timing among elements. Engaging rhythms exhibit both continuity and change, a degree of predictability, and a degree of the unexpected.

Frame			100	101	102	103	104	105	106	107
Speed	● Fast	○ Slow	○	○	○	●	●	●	●	●
Transitions	● Abrupt	○ Fluid	○	○	○	●	●	●	○	○
Activity	● Loud	○ Quiet	○	○	○	●	●	●	●	●
Elements	● Many	○ Few	○	●	●	○	●	○	○	○

5.13
Stills from the experimental
16mm film, *A Colour Box,* 1935
Len Lye

A combination of loud and quiet, linear
and curved, and soft and hard hand-
drawn markings are juxtaposed to create
a lively ebb and flow.

In motion graphics or graphic novels and other multi-panel
forms, rhythm is largely shaped through sequencing.
The order in which content is placed is critical to creating
continuity and evoking drama or tension. Moments of
visual calm or active movement and of subtlety or shock
are the result of placement, as visuals merge or suddenly
appear one after another.

Sequences manipulate the sense of time through the
duration, speed, and direction of elements. They can be
linear (progressing clearly from one idea to another),
circular or repeating (having a clear beginning and end),
or progress non-linearly or randomly among concepts
without the suggestion of a past, present, or future. Visual
notion, akin to musical scores, aids the design process
by visualizing the primary observable variables of motion:
direction, duration, pacing, and speed.

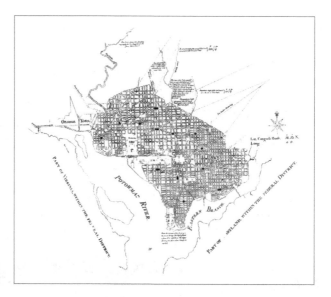

5.14
Map of Washington, DC,
1887
Designer unknown

The primary buildings housing the
legislative, judicial, and executive branches of
government are emphasized over other
governmental buildings and the city at large.

Structure describes how
the parts of a composition are
put together.

Structure is a guiding force in our lives and is often based
on naturally occurring events. The rising and setting
of the sun, the seasons, and even the phases of the moon
create structures upon which we base our routines
and plans.

Forms of all types have an underlying structure. Structure
can be natural, such as the skeletal structure of our
bodies, or human-made, such as the internal framework
of buildings. Like physical structures, visual structures
help to support and hold together the elements of a
composition. Structure is generally necessary to create
meaning and a sense of continuity. Structure allows multiple
elements to be understood as a whole.

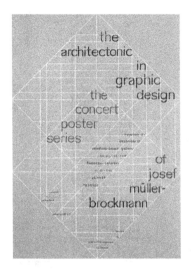

Units	3		1	0.5	1.5		4		1

5.15
Poster for an exhibition of posters,
1980
Josef Mueller-Brockmann

5.16
Poster for an
educational seminar,
1985
Wolfgang Weingart

A grid, typical of modernist design, can help create clear hierarchy, as shown in Mueller-Brockmann's work, or underlay a composition and shape visually complex interactions, as shown in Weingart's post-modernist work.

Alignment refers to the placement or grouping of visual elements in accordance with the edges or dominant interior lines of other visual elements.

Grids are a form of structure found throughout all of human activity, from city blocks and urban public transportation routes to power distribution systems.

The lines of a grid can be aligned vertically, horizontally, or diagonally. The intersections of the lines result in quadrants in which components can be placed. Grids can create an overall consistency and uniformity.

The sizes, proportions, and quantities of grid quadrants are typically based on the elements the grid will contain. A grid's structure may be apparent only through the placement of the composition's elements, or apparent as a visual element itself.

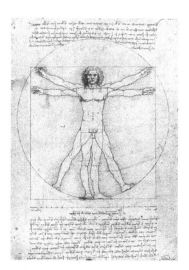

5.17
Proportional study, 15th century
Leonardo da Vinci

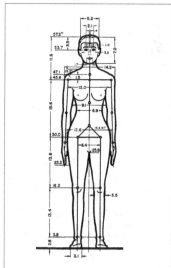

5.18
Diagram from
The Measure of Man, 1955
Henry Dreyfuss Associates

Proportion was one of the many studies of Leonardo da Vinci. He explored proportion by examining and comparing parts of the human body in relation to basic geometric shapes. His studies also sought to find a system of proportions usable for architecture. More recently, Henry Dreyfuss Associates, an industrial design firm, assembled a vast catalog of common proportions used for the design of industrial products, from chairs to automobiles.

Proportions help describe the visual forms we see each day, from buildings to household objects. They also represent the non-visual, such as the amount of time we work in a given day. Whether in visual or non-visual form, proportions can be compared, measured, and analyzed.

In visual form, the term proportion refers to the size relationship between parts of a form. Width and height can be compared to determine proportions in a two-dimensional form.

The first reference point in finding and understanding proportions is the human body. Your height (and what it allows you to see) and the length of your arms (and how far you can reach) are two continual factors that influence how you understand and interact with the world around you. The metric system, based on units of 10 (10 centimeters in a meter, 10 meters in a kilometer, and so on), relates to our 10 fingers.

5.19
Nautilus shell proportions

5.20
Shell of the
nautilus crab

The spiral form of the Nautilus shell exhibits numerical
progression while its progressive compartments exhibit the
Fibonacci series.

Fibonacci series is a relationship among numbers in which each number in the series is the sum of the two previous numbers. Any number in the series divided by the following number is approximately 0.618, and any number divided by the previous number is approximately 1.618. This ratio is often called the golden ratio and underlies geometric shapes used throughout history.
1, 1, 2, 3, 5, 8, 13, 21. . .

The points, lines, and angles of geometry are useful tools for understanding the structure of natural and human-made forms. Geometry can simplify complex visual relationships; through it, numerical ratios can be calculated and used to analyze or structure form.

Perhaps the best known ratio is found in the Fibonacci series. This group of whole numbers is named after the 16th-century Italian mathematician Leonardo of Pisa (known as Fibonacci), who advocated it as evidence of a rational order in nature. The numerical relationships in the Fibonacci series define the structure of numerous natural forms including the Nautilus shell. Such patterns illustrate that nature, on occasion, has logical, geometric, and numerically identifiable structures.

Primary
visual structure

Relationship of
golden
section rectangles

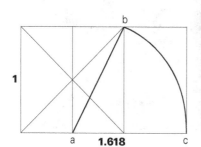

5.21
Golden section
ratio 1:1.618

5.22
Vir Heroicus Sublimis,
1950–1951
Barnett Newman

The golden section was used to structure this composition. From point (a), the length (a, b) is swung as an arc to point (c) to create a rectangle of golden section proportions.

Golden section is pleasing in and of itself—or is it pleasing because we are accustomed to its frequent use? Many common objects, such as driver's licenses, approach golden section proportions.

Perhaps the most historically significant use of geometry in the design of usable form is the golden section, also known as the golden mean or golden rectangle. The proportional relationship of the golden section has been applied both intentionally and unintentionally in two- and three-dimensional design. The golden section ratio (1:1.618) occurs in a variety of natural forms, including the Nautilus shell as expressed through the Fibonacci series.

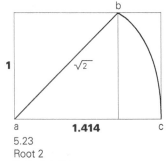

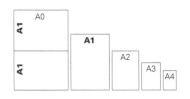

5.23
Root 2
Ratio 1:1.414

5.24
A0 (841mm x 1189mm)
Posters

A related proportion can create a visually unified grouping and allow for better communication through easy identification. From point (a), the length (a, b) is swung as an arc to point (c) to create a rectangle of root 2 proportions.

5.25
DIN relationship

Splitting or doubling a root 2 rectangle results in a rectangle of the same proportions. For example, two A1 rectangles equal an A0 rectangle. A0 (841mm x 1189mm) is the standard poster size and A4 (210mm x 297mm) is the standard letter size in most countries that use the metric system.

The root 2 rectangle is a proportional relationship similar to the golden section. While the golden section has a longer recorded history and has been used extensively in two- and three-dimensional form, the root 2 rectangle is currently more relevant and is used primarily in two-dimensional form.

Root 2 proportions have been used in paper and envelope sizes in countries around the world. This use grew out of a root 2–based system established in Germany in 1922, commonly referred to as DIN (Deutsches Institut für Normung).

A proportional standard for paper originates from the molds used in early European paper production. The root 2 rectangle can be split or multiplied to yield additional root 2 rectangles, resulting in more economical paper manufacturing, storage, and printing.

Shaping Color

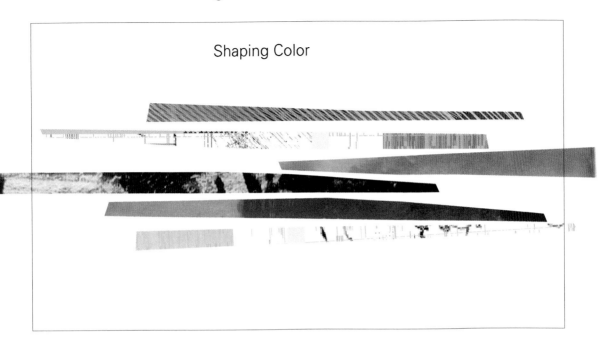

Concepts

Types
Subtractive
CMYK and Additive

Characteristics
Hue and Value
Intensity and Temperature

Interactions
Palettes
Relativity and Proportions

Applications
Space and Emphasis
Associations and Connotations

This chapter discusses the types and basic properties, associations, and applications of color.

Shaping Color

6.1
*Untitled
(Purple, White and Red)*,
1953
Mark Rothko

The translucent, loosely defined areas of color appear to float, demonstrating the power of color to create highly expressive forms.

"Colors present themselves in continuous flux, constantly related to changing neighbors and changing conditions." [18]

Josef Albers

In the late 1600s, Sir Isaac Newton experimented with simple glass prisms and found that sunlight is made up of color. Color is a property of light. Without light, there can be no color because objects have no color of their own. However, objects possess properties that absorb or reflect particular light waves, which in turn become visible to our eyes. For example, we perceive the color red when light waves of a certain frequency strike or bounce off of a surface and are transmitted to our eyes.

Our understanding of a form's color is influenced by variables, including the type and intensity of lighting on the object viewed, our distance from it, learned color associations, and surrounding colors. Thus, the definition of color is relative and dependent on cultural and physical contexts.

Shaping Color Introduction to Two-Dimensional Design

6.2
Water Lillies, 1914–1915
Claude Monet

Subtractive

Short brush strokes can create an impression of a moment. This work, based on analogous colors of green and blue, creates harmony among the elements.

Red Orange Yellow Green Blue Violet

6.3
Subtractive Color Primaries

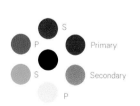

S
P Primary
S Secondary
P

6.4
Subtractive Color Wheel

There are two types of color: subtractive and additive. Subtractive color is viewed as a reflection off a surface. In subtractive color, all light waves except those containing the color we see are absorbed or "subtracted" by a surface. We see the color red when its corresponding wavelength is reflected to our eyes.

Within both subtractive and additive color types are basic colors, called primaries, from which all other colors are made. These primaries vary depending on the color's source. The relationship of primary colors to secondary colors is easily depicted through a color wheel. Secondary colors are a mixture of two primaries.

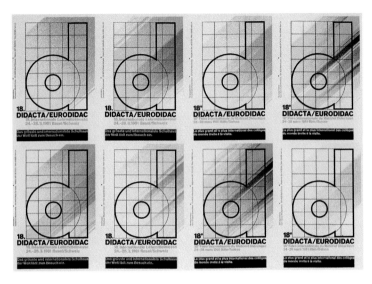

6.5
Color study, 1983
Wolfgang Weingart

CMYK (cyan, magenta, yellow, black)

6.6
Random-Access Memory web site, 2007,
John Donovan and Eric Liftin

Additive

Cyan   Magenta   Yellow   Black

6.7
CMYK and the CMYK dots of
Color study (Image 6.5)

Red-Orange   Green   Blue-Violet

6.8
Additive color primaries

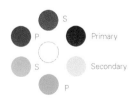

6.9
Additive color wheel

One type of subtractive color is created through pigments, whose primary colors are red, yellow, and blue. Another type of subtractive color occurs in offset printing. The colors cyan, magenta, and yellow, in conjunction with black— abbreviated as CMYK—are used in varying dot sizes and combinations to create the appearance of other colors. The individual colored dots are not physically mixed but are instead "mixed" by our eyes to form larger areas of color.

Additive color is viewed directly as light, such as that emitted by a computer monitor. Its primaries are red-orange, green, and blue-violet. When these primaries are positioned or "added" in equal amounts, white light—the source of all color—is created.

Computer monitors create the illusion of a range of colors by activating dots (pixels) to red, green, or blue in varying levels of intensity (brightness/dullness). As with CMYK, these colors are "mixed" by our eyes to create additional colors.

91

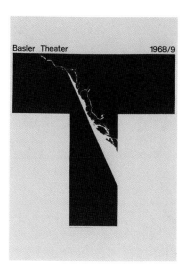

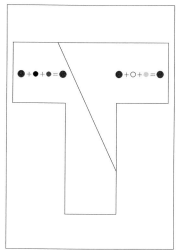

6.10
Theater poster, 1968
Armin Hofmann

A cool red on the left side and warm red on the right suggest the range of work to be shown at the theater. Approximate colors and quantities required to create the two reds are depicted in the diagram to the right.

Red   Orange Yellow Green Blue Violet
Subtractive hues

6.11
Hue

Dark   Lighter>   Light
Achromatic (black + white)

6.12
Value

Red   Lighter> Less Intense> +White
Monochromatic tints (hue + white)

Red   Darker> Less Intense> +Black
Monochromatic shades (hue + black)

6.13
Hue, value, and intensity

Subtractive and additive color has four basic qualities: hue, value, intensity, and temperature.

Hue refers to a pure color without black, or white added to it. The basic hues are red, orange, yellow, green, blue, and violet.

Value refers to the lightness or darkness of a color. You can shade a hue by adding black and tint a hue by adding white. The term achromatic applies to mixtures of black and white only, while monochromatic applies to mixtures based on shades and tints of a single hue.

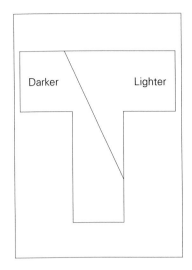

6.14
Value

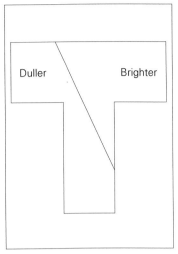

6.15
Intensity

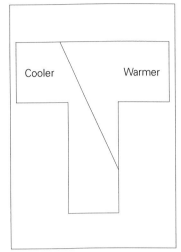

6.16
Temperature

Red   Darker> Red Less Intense>   +Violet
Adding a hue (hue + hue)

6.17
Hue, value, and intensity

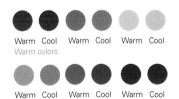

Warm Cool   Warm Cool   Warm Cool
Warm colors

Warm Cool   Warm Cool   Warm Cool
Cool colors

6.18
Hue and temperature

Intensity (or saturation) refers to the brightness or dullness of a color. A color is at full intensity or purity only when it is unmixed. A color's intensity changes when black, white, or another color is added.

Temperature refers to the relative warmth or coolness of a color. We generally think of red, orange, and yellow as warm, and blue, green, and violet as cool. But any color, even red, can be warm or cool depending on the type and amount of other colors added.

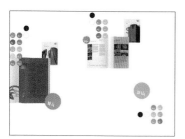

6.19
SGI Identity Manual, 1999
Patrick Cox, design director
Frank Mueller, designer
Landor

6.20
*A Sunday Afternoon
on the Island of
La Grande Jatte*, 1884
Georges Seurat

Seurat used small dots of analogous color to create an impression rather than a literal depiction by allowing the eye to optically mix the separate dots of colors. Discordant colors are a key component of the SGI identity shown to the left.

6.21
Complementary colors

6.22
Analogous colors

Color palette of *A Sunday Afternoon
on the Island of La Grande Jatte*
(Image 6.20)

Compositions can be designed using specific color palettes or color "families" to create harmony or discord as appropriate for the message.

Complementary colors are opposite from each other on the color wheel. When mixed, they create gray.

Analogous colors are adjacent to each other on the color wheel, while discordant colors are farther apart but not directly across from one another. Generally speaking, analogous colors tend to create harmony among elements, and discordant colors create instability and movement.

The red in Image 6.24 is the
same red used in *Late Reminder*,
yet it appears darker and
duller on the white background.

6.23
Late Reminder, 1953
Josef Albers

6.24
Relativity

Relativity is color in relation
to its environment. A color can be
perceived differently depending
on its surrounding colors.

3   2   1

6.25
Proportions of *Late Reminder*
(Image 6.23)

Perceptually, color is highly relative. As with other visual
elements such as size, we understand color in relation
to its environment. Color can be used to move objects
into the foreground or background, but its ability to do that
depends on the surrounding colors.

Proportions in color are defined through area while their
perceptual interactions are shaped by their value, intensity,
and temperature.

Dominant (light, bright, warm)   Subordinate (dark, dull, cool)

Soft boundary ⎯   ⎯ Receding

Hard boundary ⎯   ⎯ Advancing

Simultaneous contrast ⎯

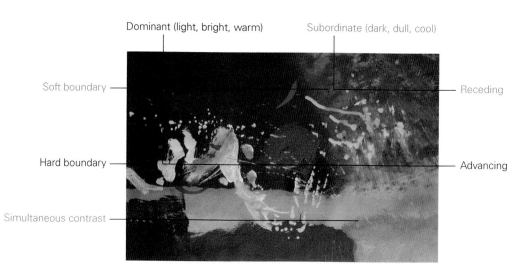

6.26
Untitled, 1965
Cameron Booth

This work creates a deep sense of space by juxtaposing colors varying in value, intensity, and temperature.

6.27
Black-and-white rendering of
Untitled, 1965
Cameron Booth

This black-and-white rendering of Booth's color work reveals color's ability to shape space and create emphasis.

Areas of color that are different in hue, value, intensity, or temperature can appear to be placed or moving forward or backward in space.

When adjacent colors vary in value, their edges are distinct or hard. When they are similar in value, their edges (or boundaries) merge and are soft. When they have the same value, their edges may appear to vibrate, a phenomenon known as simultaneous contrast.

Juxtaposed color areas of differing characteristics can create dominant or subordinate areas that, when rendered in black and white, can reveal a changed hierarchy.

6.28
Blue and red states,
Presidental election, 2004

6.29
The Rainbow Flag, 1978
Gilbert Baker

The blue represents a state that voted Democrat,
and the red a state that voted Republican. In the
rainbow flag, the red, orange, yellow, green,
blue, and violet stripes represent life, healing, sun,
serenity, harmony, and spirit, respectively.

Connotations of color can
be similar or vary across cultures.
Red, for example, connotes
danger in most cultures.
The color associated with death
and mourning is black in
the West but white in the East.

Although humans perceive color interactions similarly, our
interpretations of their meanings can vary. Most color
attributes are understood in relation to the environment in
which they exist and are interpreted through the experiences
of the designer and viewer.

We also associate color with our natural environment.
We perceive red, orange, and yellow as warm, perhaps
because of their association with fire and sunlight. Likewise,
we perceive violet, green, and blue as cool, perhaps because
of their association with sky and water.

Color can be used to convey a wealth of information
and relationships, from the black indicating gain and red
indicating loss in business, to the blue of a ribbon
awarded for excellence, to the colors used by sports teams,
corporations, and countries to create a sense of identity.

Looking Closer

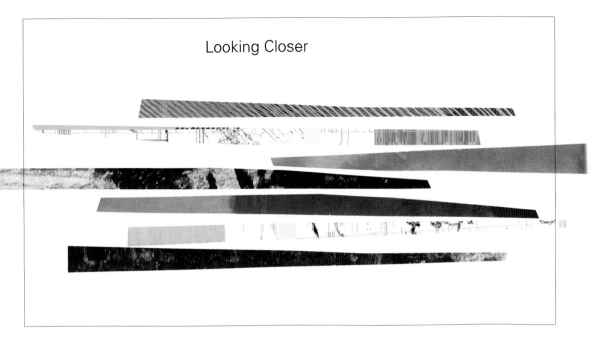

This chapter examines how select contemporary artists and designers employ a range of methodologies and media to explore social and cultural issues.

Looking Closer

Ritual	Time	Identity	Place	Power	Language
Farrell					
Green					
		Hu			
Matson					
			Morningstar		
		Napier			
					Stauffacher
The Oxford Project					

7.1
Issues of individuals and collaboratives

This in-depth exploration focuses on select individuals and collaborations that address a range of issues and create works through a variety of methodologies, media, and principles discussed earlier in this book.

Their work shows the range of contemporary two-dimensional art and design and demonstrates how boundaries among disciplines are often blurred. Collectively, the work includes typography, mixed media, painting, fiber, information design, digital interaction, printing and photography.

From Hu Hung-Shu's blending of East and West to Christy Matson's participatory tactile experiences, the pieces are unified in passionate explorations of personally meaningful issues that touch the lives of many.

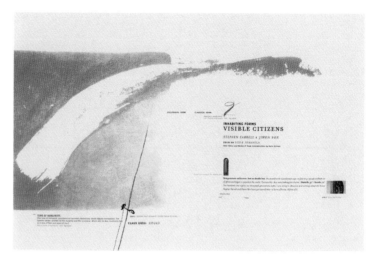

7.2
Facing pages from *Visible Citizens*, 2002
Offset print, 11" x 17"
Stephen Farrell, co-author and designer; Steve Tomasula,
co-author; and Jiwon Son, designer

Stephen Farrell is the chair of the Visual Communication program at the School of the Art Institute of Chicago. His experimental work has been published by the University of Chicago Press.

Stephen Farrell's work uses analogy to explore ways of making connections between seemingly unrelated elements. His collaborative and self-authored narratives use text to be appreciated both visually and to be read, along with conceptually related images that convey multiple meanings. Together, the text and images serve as analogies that aid viewers in the understanding of narrative subtleties and expand relationships to the subject matter.

His essay "Visible Citizens," set in the house he had recently purchased, tells a story of discovery and ritual. In the basement he discovered 14 brooms, worn with the shape of the previous tenants' hands. And in the bookcase he found a collection of 60-year-old etiquette books outlining the manners constituting cultured behavior. Farrell combined the routine of household maintenance with a striving for self-improvement and civility to create a vehicle for personal reflection and a departure point for further analysis.

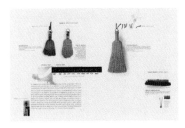
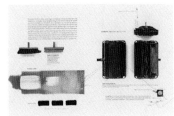

7.3
Pages from *Visible Citizens*, 2002
Stephen Farrell, co-author and
designer; Steve Tomasula,
co-author; and Jiwon Son, designer

Photographs of broom forms and gestures of sweeping are interwoven
with the ways of expressing civility as described in the etiquette books.
The typography echoes the movement of sweeping, while the image
use echoes the categorization and rules of manners. Together they express
the previous homeowners' rituals, routines, and aspirations.

Q+A with Stephen Farrell

How does analogy expand or enrich experiences?

"Analogy challenges us to bridge
the gap between two pieces of
data. This data could be anything,
from two disparate words or
pictures side by side on a page
to two large-scale topics we are
attempting to research and bring
together.

Cognitive scientists believe that
no matter how different two sets
of information seem to be at
first, our creative and deductive
capacities want to find something
that relates them: shared aspects,
correlations among the attributes,
similarities of purpose, structural parallels, nesting potentials,
cause-and-effect chains, larger,
encompassing domains, etc.
Our analogic capacity creatively
contributes to the stuff of the world,
linking elements and events into
brand new and connected ways of
understanding."[20]

How do you research and organize complicated and unfamiliar topics?

"One research method I've found
helpful was put forth by a cultural
anthropologist named Michel
Foucault. Foucault encourages
breaking down a macro-topic into
the *objects* that are part of that
topic; the pictures, terminology,
diagrams, gestures, and other
representations that are part of that
topic; the *concepts* that underlie
the topic and give the objects and
representations meaning; and
the *strategies* that use the objects
and representations to convey the
concepts."[21]

Menu
Five fried eggs (sunny-side up), hash browns, bacon strips (crisp), stack of pancakes with syrup, hot coffee, milk, and cold orange juice

Menu
Request to eat from a vending machine with family members

All plates are mineral paint, fired porcelain, and stoneware.

7.4
Oregon 6 September 2002
The Last Supper
Julie Green

7.5
Alabama 25 October 2006
The Last Supper
Julie Green

Julie Green is an associate professor of art at Oregon State University. Her work has been widely reviewed in publications including *The Chronicle of Higher Education* and on National Public Radio. To date, she has created 283 plates representing the final requests of inmates in each of the 38 states that allow the death penalty.

Julie Green's work on *The Last Supper* began after she read accounts in her local Oklahoma newspaper of death row inmates' final meal requests and moments. A brief and factual account was published the morning following the previous day's execution.

The white porcelain plates serve as the vehicle to question the use of capital punishment in a civilized society. Purchased at rummages sales and thrift shops, they are like a blank canvas for writing and visualizing the last meals of those executed. (Out of respect for the privacy of the condemned individuals, their names are withheld.)

The plates' blue color and straightforward content presentation eerily reference commemorative plates. But Green's plates represent lives, not geographical designations. She titled the work *The Last Supper* to reference to Christ's last supper before his crucifixion.

Menu
Salmon, potatoes, vegetable, green salad, desert

Menu
One bag of assorted Jolly Ranchers

Menu
Two large pepperoni and sausage pizzas, three pints of coffee ice cream, three six-packs of Coca Cola

7.6
Washington 5 January 1993
The Last Supper
Julie Green

7.7
Texas 22 October 2001
The Last Supper
Julie Green

7.8
California 23 February 1996
The Last Supper
Julie Green

Q+A with Julie Green

How did the content shape the process and outcome?

"When deciding to illustrate final meals, I tried embroidery on place mats and painting on paper before choosing mineral painting on ceramic plates. Once kiln-fired at 1,400 degrees, the plates are archival. You could eat off of them. Because new executions occur each week or two, this is an ongoing project. I plan to keep painting plates until we no longer have capital punishment."[22]

What is your role in this project?

"Andy Warhol said the artist of the future will just point. I paint to point."[23]

What is the role of your audience?

"The viewer comment book is an important element in the installation. At Copia Museum in Napa, California, the comments of 300 viewers provide an overview of our society's emotional and conflicting feelings about the death penalty."[24]

7.9
Soft, 1999
Oil on canvas, 30" x 24"
Hu Hung-Shu

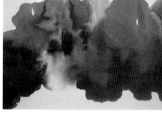

7.10
Early Spring, 1984
Oil on canvas, 44" x 36"
Hu Hung-Shu

Hu Hung-Shu was born in China and came to the United States in 1964 to attend the Cranbrook Academy of Art. He is a professor emeritus of design at the University of Iowa, a designer, painter, and sculptor, and recipient of the First Progressive Architecture Conceptual Design Competition award.

7.11
Corner Lamp, 1981
Hu Hung-Shu

Hu Hung-Shu's work is a merging of East and West, of old and new. Ancient Eastern ink wash techniques and traditional landscape painting are blended with 21st-century Western abstraction and experimental media studies.

Through this merging, he explores issues of place, including the location and role of the individual in his or her environment. Whereas traditional Eastern landscapes have a single, clearly visible horizon line, Hu's work does not. Without such a reference, viewers are required to find their own position within the work.

Building upon traditional Chinese ink work dualities such as dry versus wet, he uses very thin layers of oil to create varied effects. Through a black-and-white palette, he creates a range of subtle gray values that bring emotion and focus to compositions spontaneously and directly created on the canvas. His working method is reflective of the organic, breathing atmospheres depicted in the work.

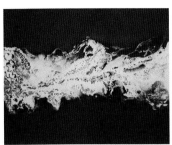

7.12
Meet, 2002
Oil on canvas, 30" x 24"
Hu Hung-Shu

7.13
Brilliant, 1999
Oil on canvas, 30" x 24"
Hu Hung-Shu

7.14
Isolated, 2003
Oil on canvas, 30" x 24"
Hu Hung-Shu

Q+A with Hu Hung-Shu

What is the relationship between your two- and three-dimensional work?

"I do not see any difference between the two. I believe a designer should not think first of a form but of an idea, and let the form follow the action of the idea. Form follows action. The three-dimensional designer must understand two-dimensional principles in the same way that a two-dimensional designer must understand three-dimensional work. Then their two-dimensional work will not appear flat, but will have space, volume, and mass. It is crucial to learn from the two-dimensional plan in order to visualize the meaning of a three-dimensional space."[25]

What defines your work?

"All of my paintings are black and white on canvas. This provides viewers greater participation in the work by allowing them to visualize colors. By painting with oil on canvas, I try to break away from traditional Chinese painting with water ink on paper. I can use my techniques to express the same effect of ink on paper in addition to many effects that inks cannot do on paper."[26]

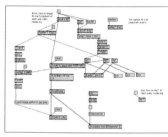

7.15
Christy Matson at the digital loom.

7.16
Digital Synesthesia, 2005
Schematic of software used to
generate the patterns.

7.17
Digital Synesthesia, 2005
Hand-jacquard woven cotton and
copper, interactive audio, 29" x 44"
Christy Matson

Christy Matson is an assistant professor at the School of the Art Institute of Chicago. She has conducted workshops in experimental weaving at the Haystack Summer Institute of the Arts.

Christy Matson's work explores sensory relationships between one's body and surrounding objects. She creates woven tactile forms, which she calls "antennae," that allow viewers to create sound through their interaction with the form.

Her work blends traditional textile processes with innovative digital technology and electronic components. She uses a digital Jacquard loom to weave cotton thread and copper wires connected to electrical circuits. The electrical circuits are attached to speakers. When the work is touched, tones are generated that correspond to the woven pattern. The result is an audience-created narrative or record of their experience with the artwork.

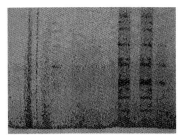

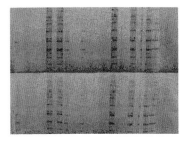

7.18
Soundw(e)ave, 2004
Detail view
Christy Matson

7.19
Soundw(e)ave, 2004
Detail view
Christy Matson

7.20
Recording sound of weaving.

Q+A with Christy Matson

How is context important in your work?

"Context always affects the way artwork is understood. I think this statement is even more relevant in reference to woven work. Experiencing the work in person gives the viewer the opportunity to understand the work as cloth. Because cloth is the closest thing to our bodies each day, the viewer is able to interpret a sense of 'understanding' that does not necessarily translate when the works are shown as photographs or video."[27]

What is the role of your audience?

"I view the tools that I use to make art as active components of the process and outcome of the work. Likewise, I think of the audience as active participants while viewing art. Although this work is not explicitly interactive, the piece is constantly changed by the viewer's engagement with it."[28]

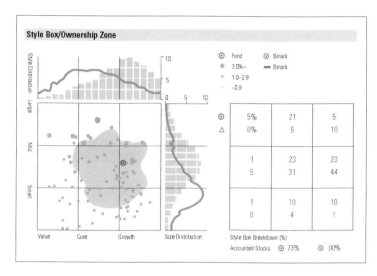

7.21
Ownership zone,
2003
Morningstar, Inc.

This diagram allows investors to locate their funds according to volatility (horizontal axis) and size (vertical axis). The flowing green area defines the investor's ownership area.

Morningstar, Inc., is a provider of independent investment research. Their information design work received an *ID* magazine merit award in 1993.

Whether in the form of maps, voting ballots, or financial documents, the design of information we encounter each day influences our ability to participate meaningfully in society.

Through information design, Morningstar, Inc., empowers others to make informed financial decisions that have a direct influence on their lives. Morningstar designers explore the problems of converting large and complex quantities of data into understandable and engaging graphic forms. Among the issues they explore is the design of effective forms that meet the audience's familiarity with conventions of diagrammatical systems, such as symbol usage and reading orders.

Their working method is based on methodically comparing versions of a design. The process moves linearly, from divergent to convergent. The multiple variations can be viewed simultaneously to reinforce choices or to move in new directions.

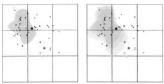

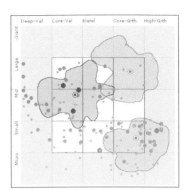

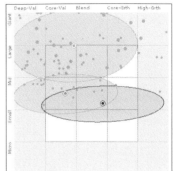

7.22
Ownership zones,
increased percentages, 2002
Morningstar, Inc.

7.23
Ownership zones,
multiple portfolios, 2003
Morningstar, Inc.

Q+A with Philip Burton
senior designer,
Morningstar, Inc.

What are the challenges of
information design?

"The main challenge is to take
what people perceive to be
complicated financial data and
make it easy for them to read
and use, to remove any
preconceived notions that the
information is too difficult to
approach. The choice of typeface,
size, weight, and style is very
important. Often it is possible
to create an illustration that
presents data in a more quickly
understandable manner."[29]

What are the visual principles
you explore?

"Jan Tschichold once said that
contrast is the most important
design principle. I would
agree. Contrast creates a
conversation among the design
elements on a page or screen.
It leads the viewer on a journey
of discovery and understanding."[30]

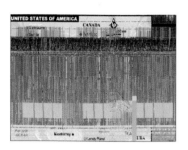
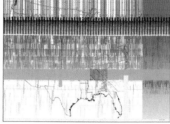
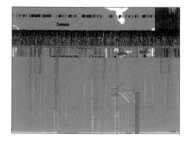

7.24
USA, 2003
(potatoland.org/word/usa)
Custom software
Mark Napier

This generative digital work transforms maps of the United States through an algorithm that reinterprets the maps' visual elements and colors into abstract shapes.

Mark Napier lives in New York City and has been commissioned by the Whitney Museum of American Art, Solomon R. Guggenheim Museum, and San Francisco Museum of Modern Art. He holds a BFA in painting and is a self-taught programmer.

Mark Napier creates experimental digital experiences that allow users to participate simultaneously in the creation of work posted online. As the designer and programmer, he acts as facilitator of a performance that requires audience participation.

One of his web sites, potatoland.org, allows users to capture imagery and text from other web sites and bring it to his site, where it is arranged randomly. Current user choices are layered upon previous user choices in a cumulative process. The result is a change in positioning and hierarchy of original content, releasing informational and persuasive items from their original purpose and context. As these new visual relationships are created among elements, our understanding of their form and function is questioned. The work is never finished, as users interact with the site, then leave as others arrive. There are only momentary records of user interaction.

  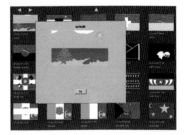

7.25
net.flag, 2002
(netflag.guggenheim.org)
Custom software
Mark Napier

This online interactive work, commissioned by the Solomon R. Guggenheim Museum, allows viewers to create their own flags by choosing and combining existing international flag symbols, patterns, and colors. The participatory process raises questions of territorial rights and geographical identity.

Q+A with Mark Napier

What are the challenges of this medium?

"Art is now an exploration of time, of processes that change over time, images that move, and objects that change. It can be enacted and reenacted, like a performance, like music. Video and film both engage time, but in a very linear fashion. These forms play out according to a fixed mechanical process and invite linear narrative. Computer-based artwork does not need to play linearly and invites a much wider range of exploration of time and non-linear experiences. The biggest challenge to this exploration is that there is no vocabulary for this form. The vocabulary is being invented as the exploration happens, which also makes the process very fascinating. We're representing time, much as painting represents space."[31]

Looking Closer Introduction to Two-Dimensional Design

7.26
*The Vico Collaboration
(Waves Murmur)*, 2004
Print, 13" x 18"
Jack Stauffacher

7.27
Jack Stauffacher with prints.

Jack Stauffacher was
born in 1920 and lives in San
Francisco, where he runs
The Greenwood Press. His work
is in the permanent collection
of the San Francisco Museum
of Modern Art.

Jack Stauffacher began printing at age 14, when he bought
a small press through the magazine *Popular Mechanics*.
He was soon printing in a small studio built in the family's
backyard. He named his press The Greenwood Press
after the street his family lived on in the San Francisco Bay
area, and today still prints under that name.

His work is a unique blend of traditional letterpress printing
and experimental design. By creating abstract compositions
using wood type, he moves type beyond its primary
and original function of text to be read in lines to forms to
be seen.

The prints are made from 65 assorted pieces of wooden
type he was given by another printer in the building where
he had reestablished his press in 1970. After an initial
selection of letters, he composes a print, and often pursues
the experiment with multiple prints that have subtle changes.

114

7.28
*Wooden Letters from
300 Broadway*, 1998
Print, 13" x 18"
Jack Stauffacher

7.29
*Wooden Letters
from 300 Broadway*, 1998
Print, 13" x 18"
Jack Stauffacher

7.30
*Wooden Letters
from 300 Broadway*, 1998
Print, 13" x 18"
Jack Stauffacher

Q+A with Jack Stauffacher

How do you balance the intuitive and methodical experimentation?

"There is no difference between 'intuitive' and 'method.' They are held together by the sum of the tools — press, wooden letters, ink, impression, paper. I have been a letterpress printer all my life and it is in this intimacy of all the elements, directly in my hands, that makes the things I do possible." [32]

What qualities does the letterpress method of printing impart to the work?

"My work is born of the Vandercook Proof letterpress. Without this tool the moving of elements could not occur. The intimacy of working directly with wooden letters, inks, and 'impression' allows me immediate and direct freedom to address the limits of the letters with which I am working." [33]

Do you visualize a composition before placing the letters in the press?

"No. My tools, the large and small wooden letters, wait in their inert state. The starting point is always the Roman letter. Roman letters present limits but also offer freedom through their abstract shapes. The composition is set in motion by the desire to reshape these graphic marks within the limits of my tools. Continually moving the elements leads to larger shapes and the final integration of the positive and negative spaces within the page." [34]

"In 1985, after 40 years of marriage, he left me for another woman. I didn't know who the woman was, but everyone else in town knew. I would have felt better if she was young and beautiful, but she wasn't." [35]

Pat Henkelman

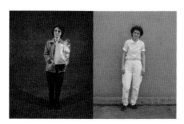

7.31
Pat Henkelman, 1984 and 2005
The Oxford Project
Peter Feldstein, photographer
Steven Bloom, writer

7.32
Darrell Lindley, 1984 and 2005
The Oxford Project
Peter Feldstein, photographer
Steven Bloom, writer

The Oxford Project is a collaboration between Peter Feldstein and Steven Bloom. Peter Feldstein is a National Endowment for the Arts grant recipient and professor emeritus of photography at the University of Iowa. Steven Bloom is a nonfiction writer and associate professor in literature at the University of Iowa.

The complete interviews of select featured residents are on pages 138–139.

In 1984, Peter Feldstein, a resident of Oxford, Iowa, began photographing the town's 676 residents. He set up a studio in an empty store on Main Street and individually captured on film the lives of his friends and neighbors. Twenty years later, he began photographing the town's residents again and this time interviewed them with his collaborator, Steven Bloom.

The resulting 670 documentary photographs are inspiring, captivating, honest, and unassuming. The backdrop is a worn construction tarp against which each person, wearing everyday clothes, is lit simply.

The interview approach is similarly unassuming and straightforward. Residents were asked to talk about anything they felt was of personal importance. The resulting visual integration of image and text captures the struggles, hopes, and changes of small-town life in the Midwest over 20 years' time.

"After basic training I was sent overseas and went through the Battle of the Bulge. I'm the last living of the first four American soldiers who liberated Buchenwald concentration camp."[36]

Jim Hoyt

7.33
Hunter Tandy, 1984 and 2005
The Oxford Project
Peter Feldstein, photographer
Steven Bloom, writer

7.34
Jim Hoyt, 1984 and 2005
The Oxford Project
Peter Feldstein, photographer
Steven Bloom, writer

7.35
Violet Reihman, 1984 and 2005
The Oxford Project
Peter Feldstein, photographer
Steven Bloom, writer

Q+A with Peter Feldstein

What is your role in this project?

"I suppose I'm more of a mediator than anything else. I try to make as little comment through the photographs as possible. I want the photographs, and Steve feels the same about the text, to be as democratic as possible. I hope to make the frame like a stage upon which my neighbors can act themselves out."[37]

How has this project changed you?

"I'm learning a lot about human resilience and how strong people are in facing life's problems and tragedies through strength of character and religious belief. I'm very interested in how different individuals can process the same information so differently."[38]

Timeline

The design timeline on the following pages will help you contextualize the concepts discussed earlier in this book. The timeline contains the primary art and design movements, philosophical thoughts and trends, and significant political and social events of the past 100 years.

From the early 20th century activism of Dada to contemporary and expansive forms of message-making, the timeline illustrates how design both influences and is influenced by changes in thought, social conditions, world events, and technology.

Timeline

Untitled
(Pole Vaulter),
1936,
Alexander Rodchenko

*Counter-
Composition VIII*,
1924,
Theo van Doesburg

Poster for the Rural
Electrification Administration,
1937,
Lester Beall

Cover for
The Dada Painters,
1951,
Paul Rand

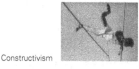

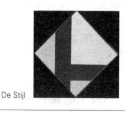

Constructivism   De Stijl   WPA   Modernism

1900	1910	1920	1930	1940	1950

Movements

Cubism
(1907–1914)

Dada
(1916–1920)

Modernism
(1919–)

Bauhaus
(1919–1933)

WPA
(1935–1943)

International Typographic Style
(1945–1970)

Constructivism
(1915–1940)

De Stijl
(1917–1931)

Social Realism
(1930–1945)

Abstract Expressionism
(1945–1970)

Theories

Structuralism
Saussure (1916–)

Semiotics
Morris (1938–)

Arts

Armory Show
New York City (1913)

Molded Plywood Chair
Ray and Charles Eames (1946)

Rashomon
Akira Kurosawa (1950)

Writings

The Interpretation of Dreams
Sigmund Freud (1900)

Tender Buttons
Gertrude Stein (1912)

Avant-Garde and Kitsch
Clement Greenberg (1939)

Changes

Einstein's theory of
relativity (1905)

19th Amendment gives
American women the right to vote (1920)

American
suburbanization (1947–)

Events

World War I
(1914–1918)

World War II
(1940–1945)

Treaty of Versailles ends
World War I (1918)

Atomic bombs dropped on
Hiroshima and Nagasaki (1945)

United Nations
founded (1945)

Advancements

First transistor patent
issued (1928)

Early television
broadcasts (1940)

First self-sustaining nuclear
chain reaction (1942)

Timeline

Airport:
Cat Paws,
1974,
Robert Rauschenberg

Poster for an
educational seminar,
1985,
Wolfgang Weingart

Poster for an academic
program,
1984,
Jeff Keedy

Potatoland
(potatoland.org),
2007,
Mark Napier

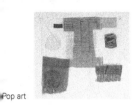

Pop art   Post-
                                 modernism   Deconstructive
                                                              typography   New media

1960	1970	1980	1990	2000	+

Pop art   Post-modernism   New media   Digital/deconstructive typography
(1950–1970)   (1970s–)   (1980s–)   (1980s–)

Conceptual art   Identity design   Artists' books   Pictorial art
(1960s–)   (1960s–)   (1970s–)   (1980s–)

Post-structuralism   Post-modernism/deconstruction   Contemporary feminism/queer theory
Foucault (1965–)   Derrida (1967–)   Butler (1990–)

Guggenheim Museum   *Music in Twelve Parts*   Mapplethorpe/Serrano/NEA   *Cremaster 1*
Frank Lloyd Wright (1959)   Philip Glass (1971)   Censorship Controversy (1989–1990) Matthew Barney (1996)

First Things First   *The Medium is the Massage*   *Learning from Las Vegas*   *Emigré*
manifesto (1964)   McLuhan and Fiore (1967)   Venturi, Izenour, and Brown (1977)   (1984–2005)

March on Washington, DC   Globalization   EU ratifies Kyoto Protocol
for civil rights (1963)   accelerates (1980s–)   on climate change (1990)

Vietnam War   Cold War ends   9/11 Terrorism
(1963–1975)   (1989)   (2001)

President Kennedy   Rev. Martin Luther King and
assassinated (1963)   Robert F. Kennedy assassinated (1968)

Russian cosmonaut Yuri Gagarin   Apple Macintosh   Public Internet   Human genome
first human in space (1961)   introduced (1984)   emerges (1993)   decoded (2000)

121

Movements Definitions and Examples

The art and design movements represented in this
book are defined on the following pages. Each definition
is accompanied by the names of key individuals or
collaborations shown earlier.

These are not the only movements of the 20th and early
21st century; they are among the most dominant and
influential. Some of the movements encompass other
movements. For example, modernism includes De Stijl,
Abstract Expressionism, and identity design, among
others. Further, many of the individual artists and designers
can be associated with more than one movement.

Each movement's beginning date is based on significant
exhibitions, manifesto publication dates, identification by
a critic of the time, or a technological advancement that
facilitated activity. The introduction of the Apple Macintosh
computer in 1984, for instance, resulted in an explosion
of digital font design and experimental typography.
A movement's ending date is based on institutional closings,
such as Bauhaus in 1933; a disbanding of participants; or
the passing of a key individual.

Movements Definitions and Examples

43
89
120
Abstract expressionism (1945–1970), which originated in New York City, was an art movement primarily of non-representational painting. Although the movement included a wide range of styles, it was typically noted for its use of large canvases and an intuitive approach to expression.
Jackson Pollock
Mark Rothko

20
27
121
Artists' books are limited-edition, often self-authored books whose content and design are outside mainstream book publishing. They typically employ experimental binding techniques, may combine traditional printing methods with digital means, and use typography meant to be viewed and appreciated as well as to be read. Contemporary artists' books have gained increased recognition since the 1970s.
Warren Lehrer
Heejin Kim

95
120
Bauhaus (1919–1933) was a highly influential German design school that led the modernist movement before the Nazis closed it for subversion. The curriculum stressed mass-produced objects that retained a sense of individuality. Geometry, simplicity, and functionality typified the work of the students and instructors, many of whom immigrated to the United States and became key figures in design.
Josef Albers

28
Black Mountain College (1933–1956) was an experimental liberal arts school in North Carolina that fostered a generation of avant-garde artists and writers. John Cage and Josef Albers were among the faculty, and Robert Rauschenberg was a student.
Robert Rauschenberg

104
105
121
Conceptual art describes a broad range of art created since the 1960s that stresses a form's concept and message, often through non-traditional means.
Julie Green

120
Constructivism (1915–1940) was primarily a Russian movement in graphic design, painting, photography, and sculpture. Geometric abstraction and juxtapositions of image and type departed from the prevailing representational forms of the time, largely for the promotion of socialist causes.
Alexander Rodchenko

Movements Definitions and Examples

74
120
Cubism (1907–1914) was an art movement influenced by the directness and simplicity of primitive art and by new thinking in philosophy and the sciences that questioned the status quo. The movement sought new ways of depiction, such as the use of abstraction, geometric planes, and multiple views to portray a single object.
Pablo Picasso

34
120
Dada (1916–1920) was a movement in art, literature, and theater active throughout Europe and New York City primarily during World War I. Participants in the movement questioned the conventions of the time and believed those in power were responsible for the war. Montages of found imagery and work based on chance were characteristic of Dada activity. The term Dada is a euphuism for "anti-art," although the origin of the word is debated.
Hannah Hoch

120
De Stijl (1917–1931) was a Dutch movement that crossed fine art and applied design, including architecture. The movement was characterized by geometric forms of primary colors, black, and white juxtaposed through simple grid structures. Through the reduced palette, participants sought to express spiritual harmony and to merge art and design. *De Stijl* translated from Dutch means "the style."
Theo van Doesburg

102
103
121
Digital/deconstructive typography (1980s–) explores symbolic representations and non-linear reading orders through typography meant to be seen as well as to be read. It is shaped by the Post-Modernist theories of Michel Foucault and others who examined embedded codes as a way of expanding interpretation.
Stephen Farrell
Jeff Keedy

42
DIY (do it yourself) (1980s–) is a cross-disciplinary movement whose followers engage in design without professional aid. Although the idea of doing it yourself is not new, the DIY movement has been enhanced by the computer, which allows virtually anyone to create and distribute content. The movement has received growing attention and has been the subject of several recent exhibitions.
Do It Yourself Exhibition

60
63
121
Identity design (1960s–) is a branch of graphic design that creates the visual forms used in marketing strategies for corporations or non-profit organizations. These forms may include simple "look and feel" designs, such as symbols; guidelines for an identity's components, such as its color palette and usage rules; or applications such as web sites and signage.
Landor
Paul Rand

81
92
120
International Typographic Style (1945–1970) is a form of graphic design that originated in Switzerland. It emphasized common modernism traits of simplicity, clarity, and objectivity. Asymmetry, sans-serif fonts, and clearly visible compositional structures were commonly employed.
Josef Mueller-Brockmann
Armin Hofmann

18
43
63
120
Modernism (1919–) refers to movements in art, architecture, design, music, literature, and philosophy that, in general, express beliefs in progress, function over decoration, and the designer as the director of experiences. Rooted in the rejection of prevailing conventions deemed corrupt by some and the need to better express contemporary issues, Modernism evolved into a widely accepted approach.
Jackson Pollock (Abstract Expressionism)
Paul Rand (identity design)
Theo van Doesburg (De Stijl)

59
108
109
112
113
121
New media is a broad term referring to art created through a computer or other electronic means. Such work can be experienced through the Internet and assume multiple forms, including video and interactive or printed digital imagery. The term emerged in the 1980s.
Christy Matson
Mark Napier
Lisa Strausfeld

78
121
Pop Art (1950–1970) explored the influence and value of popular mass culture. Such work used images from advertisements, comics, and packaging as subject matter. The resulting work served as a commentary on the role of mass-disseminated images in society and the ability of mediated experiences to shape culture.
Andy Warhol

Movements Definitions and Examples

8   **Post-Modernism** (1970s–) is a movement active across many disciplines
9   that extends, or in some cases completely rejects Modernism.
18   Like Modernism, the movement has taken many forms, but it generally
72   embraces ambiguity over clarity, symbolic content over overt presentation,
121 or audience participation over passive viewing.
April Greiman (new media/digital deconstructive typography)
Jeff Wall (pictorial art)
Guerrilla stickers (street art)

57   **Public art** (1960s–) is art designed for and placed (officially) in a public
space. The work often intrudes upon and changes established patterns of
communication, interaction, or movement. In the broadest sense, public
art has a long tradition and contemporary work has benefited by Percent
for Art programs, which set aside a percentage of public space construction
costs for art and design work.
Michele Oka Doner

20   **Social activism** describes actions taken to create social change. It is
often political and may be deliberately confrontational. The work includes
unofficial forms such as street art as well as official, mainstream forms.
Activism through design has always existed.
Guerrilla Girls

58   **Social realism** (1930–1945) was a movement that depicted the struggle of
120 the everyday life of the working class and the benefits of hard work. Murals
and representational depictions were common.
Diego Rivera

72   **Street art** (1960s–) is art designed for and placed (unofficially) in a public
space. It includes graffiti, stickers, stencils, and street posters. Messages
range from expressions of identity and terriority to those political in nature.
Placed on objects such as traffic signs and mailboxes, street art is largely
illegal yet has been recognized for decades as an influential art form.
Guerrilla stickers

62   **Works Progress Administration (WPA) Art** (1935–1943) was art
120 commissioned by the U.S. Works Progress Administration, a federal project
enacted to lift the country out of the Depression. Sacrifice for the common
good, often expressed through heroic imagery, was a standard theme.
Lester Beall

Terms

7   **Aesthetics** is a branch of philosophy that examines the nature of sensory perception and the experience and definition of beauty.

81   **Alignment** refers to the placement or grouping of visual elements in accordance with the edges or dominant interior lines of other visual elements.

28   **Appropriation** is the adoption of popular cultural imagery, conventions, visual languages, or traditions for use often unrelated to the original context. Commentary and persuasion are two common motives.

49   **Attribute lists** are a collection of adjectives that describe a work's visual expression. Created early in the problem solving process, they can direct all visual decision making, including the choice of color palettes or fonts.

17   **Audience** refers to the receiver(s) of a message. An audience can be targeted or open-ended, narrow or broad, and treated as passive observers or active participants.

28   **Coding and decoding** refer to the act of putting together and analytically taking apart a message. Codes can be visual signifiers that, when decoded, yield new understanding.

42   **Collaboration** is a process between two or more people who work together to achieve common goals.

25   **Computer-mediated communication (CMC)** refers to computer-based communication, including e-mail and instant messaging. Research suggests that, in some situations, CMC can be as effective as face-to-face interaction.

6   **Concept** is an idea that serves as the basis of a work. All work has an underlying concept that is open to interpretation, whether ambiguous, obscure, or self-evident.

97   **Connotations** of color can be similar or vary across cultures. Red, for example, connotes danger in most cultures. The color associated with death and mourning is black in the West but white in the East.

Terms

5 **Context** refers to the physical location or cultural environment in which a work exists, and influences the viewer's or user's interpretation of the work's message or function. For example, the letter X on a sidewalk may designate an excavation site for a public utility; on a greeting card it may represent a kiss and an expression of affection (e.g., XOXO); and on a shopping list it may indicate that an item was found.

75 **Contrast** refers to differences among elements and their degree of conflict or discord. These differences are often described in relative terms, such as high contrast and low contrast.

62 **Cropping** refers to the way an element that appears to extend beyond the compositional boundaries is cut off at the frame edge.

28 **Denotation and connotation** relate to the meaning of objects. Denotation refers to the physical appearance of an object: a square is a shape with four equal sides. Connotation refers to an interpretation of an object: a square can suggest neutrality or stability.

4 **Design** is a form's visual appearance, message, and purpose. In a broad sense, this includes its context, targeted audience, and media, which collectively describe its form and function. Design can be applied (such as graphic design) or non-applied (such as fine art).

47 **Divergent and convergent thinking** refers to thinking broadly (divergent) to create multiple options and then focusing (convergent) on select concepts based on deductive reasoning and formed conclusions. Problem-solving explorations move from the divergent to the convergent throughout the creative process; the interplay between the two generates and refines options.

83 **Fibonacci series** is a relationship among numbers, in which each number in the series is the sum of the two previous numbers. Any number in the series divided by the following number is approximately 0.618, and any number divided by the previous number is approximately 1.618. This ratio is often called the golden ratio and underlies geometric shapes used throughout history. 1, 1, 2, 3, 5, 8, 13, 21. . .

8 **Form** has numerous meanings, many derived from the Latin word *forma*, which is based on the Greek words for shape, structure, and idea.

Terms

9 **Function** is a form's practical, spiritual, cultural, or personal use. In two-dimensional design, function is synonymous with purpose, with a form's intent. This includes an evaluation of why the form was created, its audience, how it will be used, and what it will do.

73 **Generative work** builds upon itself and expands in the process. It is a less linear or methodical form of theme and variation in that all aspects of the process are led by the preceding result but open to incremental or drastic change.

84 **Golden section** is pleasing in and of itself — or is it pleasing because we are accustomed to its frequent use? Many common objects, such as driver's licenses, approach golden section proportions.

76 **Hierarchy** refers to the levels of emphasis or importance in a composition. From business to sports, organized human expressions and activities that join people in reaching common goals exhibit some degree of hierarchy.

6 **Idea** is an image or thought formed in the mind. Ideation is the process of forming and relating ideas.

11 **Interpretation** is the translation of a form's message through the filters of one's perspective. Interpretation derives meaning and understanding.

43 **Intuition** refers to decision making based on instinct or innate knowledge.

62 **Juxtaposition** refers to the positioning of contrasting elements such as hard and soft, and contrasting concepts such as weak and strong.

44 **Maslow's Hierarchy of Needs** are self-actualization (creativity), esteem (respect and achievement), love (belonging and intimacy), safety (income and relationships), and physiological (food and shelter) — all strategic marketing targets.

11 **Meaning** is derived intent, purpose, or information of a message, and is influenced by the viewer's or user's experiences and abilities.

29 **Metaphors** are the use of a word or image to suggest comparison to another object or concept.

Terms

40   **Methodology** is a select grouping of concepts, ideas, processes, or theories used to guide an investigation and its underlying assumptions. Method refers to specific processes or sequences of events used by a methodology.

27   **Narratives** are stories told by a narrator. Unlike a news account, in which groups of facts or observations are reported, a narrative is an interwoven collection of memories, facts, and observations. The word *narrative* originates from the Latin *narrare*, to recount.

78   **Pattern** is created through the repetition of individual elements to form a larger grouping.

46   **Problem solving** has four basic components: learning, identifying, generating, and implementing. It is most effective when the process facilitates searching as well as solving by expanding a problem's posed conditions, such as constraints or preconceived outcomes.

41   **Process** refers to a sequence of events that culminate in a result. Processes occur throughout nature and in human activity, such as in the process of learning. Many processes are recurring and repeatable, although the results may differ.

21   **Propaganda** is a form of persuasive messaging in which information is presented for the purpose of gaining or maintaining power and control. The extent to which generally accepted truths are distorted is open to interpretation and point of view.

82   **Proportion** was one of the many studies of Leonardo da Vinci. He explored proportion by examining and comparing parts of the human body in relation to basic geometric shapes. His studies also sought to find a system of proportions usable for architecture. More recently, Henry Dreyfuss Associates, an industrial design firm, assembled a vast catalog of common proportions used for the design of industrial products, from chairs to automobiles.

5   **Purpose** refers to a design's goal or guiding principles and can be determined by an agenda, objective, or strategy.

95   **Relativity** is color in relation to its environment. A color can be perceived differently depending on its surrounding colors.

Terms

37   **Representation** is created through the use of *symbols* in which a sign's meaning is culturally agreed upon, such as the letters "XING" to abbreviate the word "crossing"; *icons* in which a sign's meaning is derived from resemblance to an object, such as the walking pedestrian depicted on a pedestrian crossing sign; and *indexes* in which a sign's meaning is derived through reasoning and association, such as two parallel lines surrounding a pedestrian icon to indicate a crosswalk and safety zone.

60   **Scale** refers to the relative size relationship among objects.

26   **Signals and cues** are visual or auditory indicators. A signal indicates the expectation that an action will be performed, whereas a cue indicates that an action has been completed.

45   **Strategy** is a plan of action designed to achieve a particular goal or goals. Effective strategies attempt to anticipate changing conditions such as user traits or to redefine existing relationships among audiences, products, and messages.

80   **Structure** describes how the parts of a composition are put together.

16   **Theory** describes groupings of ideas that seek to explain a phenomenon, guide investigation, or shape interpretation.

48   **Thinking maps** are based on related descriptive words chosen by free association and placed in an expanding fashion to further understanding of the center word.

72   **Vernacular design** is work done by those without formal design training that often expresses regional styles and is made with inexpensive materials.

72   **Visual language** is a mode of expression. It is a combination of style, visual elements, and media.

48   **Visualization matrices** use images and words as an aid to understanding and creating visuals. Common categories include description (what is it?), identification (what defines it?), and operation (how does it work?).

11   **Voice** is the combination of unique perspective and individual expression. It refers to the choice and use of visual principles and media, and to the methods employed in presenting ideas, desires, and opinions.

Study Questions Chapter Concepts

Chapter 1
Thinking Broadly

Analyze the space you're in now. Who is the audience, what is the purpose of the space, what is emphasized (form or function), and what might be the underlying design concept?

Choose one work in this book that best represents your aspirations, another that represents your personality, and another that represents your belief system. Describe how each example expresses these aspects of yourself.

What are the criteria you use to evaluate design (e.g., ability to communicate information, ability to inspire, presentation of a social issue)? Which of these do you regard as the highest calling of design?

How is two-dimensional design related to sculpture and architecture?

Chapter 2
Sending and Receiving Messages

Apply the basic questions asked by each of the six viewpoints for critiquing messages (see page 19) to a work in the book. What additional questions did the process raise about the chosen work?

Design an additional letter (upper and lower case) for the Roman alphabet and place it within the existing 26 upper and lower case letters.
How does your new letter conform to the alphabet's visual principles yet display originality?

List the visual and audible signals and cues you receive when interacting with an ATM or vending machine. Which signals and cues are critical, unnecessary, cross-cultural, or effective?

What metaphor or analogy have you recently used to explain a concept? How did you choose your metaphor or analogy, and how was it part of a larger presentation?

Study Questions Chapter Concepts

Chapter 3
Applying Theories and Methodologies

Describe how a situation of user choice, audience participation, or collaboration was critical to a meaningful experience.

Describe the process you undertook to leave your home this morning. Was it planned, linear, structured, or effective?

Describe a problem you encountered recently and the process you used to solve it.

Create one or more thinking maps and visualization matrices to help describe what billboards, tattoos, and web sites have in common.

Chapter 4
Exploring Visual Components

How does the size of everyday objects influence how you interpret or interact with them?

Find a form that has active and passive space. Describe how the use of space contributes to its message.

Find a work in this book that has a strong sense of beginning, middle, and end (or foreground, middle ground, and background), and another work that does not. How do the respective approaches convey their messages?

Choose one work in this book and rate the visual weight of its components. How does the relative weight of each component dictate reading/viewing order and emphasis?

Chapter 5
Composing Visually

In your own words, make a list of the visual languages you encountered today. Which are informative and which are persuasive? Which have limited social value and which benefit society?

Choose an image that represents your life's structure (routine and habits) or journey (e.g., geographical) and describe why.

Cut apart and reassemble a found package such as a cereal box, and alter its attributes and focus (e.g., its identification, description, or operation) by changing its hierarchy and structure.

Which compositional principle or interaction do you consider the most important in shaping interpretation? Why?

Chapter 6
Shaping Color

Choose a color in a piece of clothing you're currently wearing. How can it become lighter or darker, brighter or duller, warmer or cooler? How would a change alter your perception of yourself?

What are the primary methods of creating emphasis with a color?

Describe the color palettes in the environment along your commute. What are their proportions and what connotations do they convey?

What coded color usages do you encounter daily? How do they contribute to the experience?

Chapter 7
Looking Closer

What do the select artists, designers, and writers have in common?

How are the principles of theme and variation, choices of visual language, and expression of voice used?

Choose one body of work and describe the issues, methodology, and theoretical approach of the artist or designer.

For the same body of work, describe its use of texture, color, balance, direction, position, space, rhythm, and hierarchy.

Pat Henkelman

I get up at 5AM. My son — he works as a prison guard — stops by for breakfast every morning. He usually wants cream of wheat or oatmeal. Then I say my morning prayers, take a bath, and eat breakfast. After that, I clean houses. I come home and have lunch, usually a sandwich and a cup of green tea. I watch TV, usually CNN. Sometimes I take a nap.

In 1940, Harry and I were working at a bee factory in Harlan, and when I came back from lunch one day, he was filling my jars. That night we met at the county fair and had our picture taken, and that was that.

In 1985, after 40 years of marriage, he left me for another woman. I didn't know who the woman was, but everyone else in town knew. I would have felt better if she was young and beautiful, but she wasn't. They used to play euchre at the legion hall. My faith helped me get through. I don't have malice or anger. You have to forgive. For a while I thought I hated him. But that stopped.

Jesus died to suffer for our sins, but you're still responsible for the sins you commit. I think the instant you die, you step out of your body. You have to be perfect to go to heaven. If you're not you go to purgatory. I suppose some people like Mother Teresa might go directly to heaven, but almost everyone else goes to purgatory.

There used to be a hat store in town. I wish it still was here. I love hats.

Darrell Lindley

I shoot 'em, bleed 'em, then skin 'em. I do hogs, cattle, goats, buffalo, and sheep. I use a .22 magnum. After I shoot 'em, I cut their throats. Hogs, I stick 'em underneath in their brisket. Tomorrow I'm going to do four hogs. That'll take me four hours. Hogs, I get 24 dollars a piece. Cattle is 50 dollars, plus the hide. There was a time when I'd work six days a week. I had customers in seven counties. I used to do five, six thousand heads a year.

One thing I do, if kids are around is I cut out the eye (it's a little smaller than a golf ball), and I swish it around my mouth. The kids can't believe that. Then I give the eyeball to the health teacher at the school so the kids can dissect it.

The invasion of Iraq was very foolish. We never should've gone there. A just war is one thing, but this war isn't just. Bush isn't honest. He's an idiot and a coward.

Disappointments? I don't have a lot. I wish I had charged people more, maybe then I'd have more money now.

I like to fish. Usually I catch one big catfish every summer.

Jim Hoyt

My father worked for the Rock Island Railroad and my mother was a rural schoolteacher. I went from kindergarten through twelfth grade in the same building. My biggest achievement was winning the Johnson County Spelling Bee in 1939. I was in the eighth grade and I still remember the word I spelled correctly: archive.

After basic training I was sent overseas and went through the Battle of the Bulge. I'm the last living of the first four American soldiers who liberated Buchenwald concentration camp.

There were thousands of bodies piled high. I saw hearts that had

been taken from live people in medical experiments. They said a wife of one of the SS officers— they called her the Bitch of Buchenwald — saw a tattoo she liked on the arm of a prisoner, and then had the skin made into a lampshade. I saw that, too.

Seeing these things, it changes you. I was a kid. Des Moines had been the furthest I'd ever been from home. I have post-traumatic-stress syndrome. I still have horrific dreams. Usually someone needs help and I can't help them. I'm in a situation where I'm trapped and I can't get out. My oldest son, who was awarded the Purple Heart for service in Vietnam, suffers from the same thing.

I go to a group therapy session every week at the VA hospital and we talk about what each of us is going through. For the 50 year anniversary of the liberation of Buchenwald, they asked me to return. They would've paid for the whole thing. But I said no. I didn't want to bring back those memories.

If I had to do it over again, I would have pushed to be a psychologist — if for no other reason than to understand myself better.

Violet Reihman

I was born in Oxford. My father was a blacksmith.

I have neuropathy. It's like a real bad case of arthritis. I try to get by with a cane, but it's not easy. Tomorrow we're going to Wal-Mart to talk to an insurance man about the new Medicare drug plans. I hope we'll get some answers.

Two of our sons were wounded in Vietnam. One had his femur shot off, the other was shot in the shoulder. If my boys were of draft age today, we'd leave and move to Canada. We've got the worst president. We're so far in debt now I don't know how we're ever going to get back to normal.

This is the only house we've been in. Lived here for 61 years. We paid $1,650 for our home back in 1944.

Once a month we go to Tama to play bingo and the slots. We don't take much money.

I have my daily devotions. As long as you believe in God and go to church, that's all that's necessary.

Baking is good for me. I like to make kolaches.

Endnotes

Chapter 1
Thinking Broadly

1
Norman Potter, *What Is a Designer: Things, Places, Messages* (London: Hyphen Press, 1980), 13.
2
Garland Kirkpatrick, "A Noticeable Absence," *Sphere* 1, no. 1, (1990): 10.
3
Meredith Davis and Robin Moore, *Education through Design: Middle School Curriculum.* (Raleigh: North Carolina Arts Council, 1993), 19.
4
Interview with Peter Feldstein July, 2007

Chapter 2
Sending and Receiving Messages

5
Katie Salen and Eric Zimmerman, *Rules of Play: Game Design Fundamentals* (Cambridge, MA: MIT Press, 2004), 41.
6
Werner J. Severin and James W. Tankard, Jr. *Communication Theories: Origins, Methods and Uses* (New York: Hastings House Publishers, 1970), 6.
7
Andrew Blauvelt, "Rashomon Meets Superman in the Language Machine," *New Media, New Narratives?*, ed. Louise Sandhaus, editor (Chicago: American Center for Design, 2000), 36.
8
Marshall McLuhan and Quentin Fiore, *The Medium is the Massage* (New York: Bantam Books, 1967), 8.
9
Donald Norman, *The Psychology of Everyday Things* (New York: Basic Books, 1988), 9–11, 87–92.

Endnotes

**Chapter 3
Applying Theories and
Methodologies**

10
Mario Bellini (lecture,
International Design Conference
at Aspen, CO,1989).
11
Rudolf Arnheim, "Gestalt
Psychology and Artistic Form,"
in *Aspects of Form*, ed. Lancelot
Law Whyte (Bloomington,
Indiana: Indiana University Press,
1966), 204–205.
12
David Diamond, "The Way We
Live Now: Questions for Linus
Torvalds; The Sharer," *The New
York Times Magazine*, September
28, 2003, 23.
13
Chuck Carlson, Tim Hartford, and
Carl Wohlt, *The Graphic Design
Handbook for Business* (Chicago:
American Institute of Graphic Arts
[AIGA], 1995), 12.

**Chapter 4
Exploring Visual Components**

14
Sharon Wood, "He's Got a Thing
for Bridges." *The Oregonian*,
June 24, 1996, C1.

**Chapter 5
Composing Visually**

15
Horatio Greenough, *The Travels,
Observations, and Experiences
of a Yankee Stonecutter* (New
York: G. P. Putnam and Company,
1852).
16
Arthur Drexler, *Ludwig Mies Van
der Rohe* (New York: George
Braziller, 1960), 31.
17
Robert Venturi, *Complexity and
Contradiction in Architecture*.
(New York: Museum of Modern
Art, 1967), 17.

**Chapter 6
Shaping Color**

18
Josef Albers, *The Interaction
of Color* (New Haven, CT: Yale
University Press, 1963), 5.

**Chapter 7
Looking Closer**

19
Interview with Julie Green
June, 2007
20 21
Interview with Stephen Farrell
August, 2007
22 23 24
Interview with Julie Green
August, 2007
25 26
Interview with Hu Hung-Shu
July, 2007
27 28
Interview with Christy Matson
July, 2007
29 30
Interview with Philip Burton
September, 2007
31
Interview with Mark Napier
August, 2007
32 33 34
Interview with Jack Stauffacher
September, 2007
35 36 37 38
Interview with Peter Feldstein
July, 2007

Bibliography

Chapter 1
Thinking Broadly

Berger, John. *Ways of Seeing*. New York: Viking, 1972.

Dondis, Donis. *A Primer of Visual Literacy*. Cambridge, MA: MIT Press, 1972.

Meggs, Philip and Alston W. Purvis. *A History of Graphic Design*, 4th ed. New York: John Wiley and Sons, 2005.

Sayre, Henry. *A World of Art*. New York: Prentice Hall, 2004.

www.sfmoma.org/msoma/index. html

Chapter 2
Sending and Receiving Messages

Harrison, Charles and Paul Wood, editors. *Art in Theory 1900–2000: An Anthology of Changing Ideas*. Malden, MA: Blackwell, 2002.

Lupton, Ellen and J. Abbott Miller. *Design, Writing, Research*. New York: Kiosk, 1996.

Lechte, John. *Fifty Key Contemporary Thinkers: From Structuralism to Postmodernity*. London: Routledge, 1994.

Lupton, Ellen. *Thinking with Type*. New York: Princeton Architectural Press, 2007.

McLuhan, Marshall and Quentin Fiore. *The Medium is the Massage*. New York: Bantam Books, 1967.

Nielsen, Jakob. *Designing Web Usability: The Practice of Simplicity*. Indianapolis: New Riders, 1999.

www.aiga.org/content.cfm/voice

Bibliography

Chapter 3
Applying Theories and Methodologies

Arnheim, Rudolf. *Art and Visual Perception: A Psychology of the Creative Eye.* Berkeley: University of California Press, 1974.

Koberg, Don and Jim Bagnall. *The Universal Traveler.* Los Altos, CA: William Kaufmann, 1976.

Lidwell, William, Kritina Holden, and Jill Butler. *Universal Principles of Design.* Beverly, MA: Rockport, 2003.

Norman, Donald. *The Psychology of Everyday Things.* New York: Basic Books, 1988.

Tufte, Edward R. *The Visual Display of Quantitative Information.* Cheshire, CT: Graphics Press, 1983.

Wurman, Richard Saul. *Information Anxiety.* New York: Doubleday, 1991.

Chapter 4
Exploring Visual Components

Maier, Manfred. *Basic Principles of Design.* New York: Van Nostrand Reinhold, 1977.

Wong, Wucius. *Principles of Two-Dimensional Design.* New York: Van Nostrand Reinhold, 1972.

Chapter 5
Composing Visually

Hofmann, Armin. *Graphic Design Manual.* New York: Van Nostrand Reinhold, 1965.

Mueller-Brockmann. Josef. *Grid Systems in Graphic Design.* Niederteufen, Switzerland: Arthur Niggli, 1961.

Chapter 6
Shaping Color

Albers, Josef. *Interaction of Color.* New Haven, CT: Yale University Press, 1963.

Itten, Johannes. *The Elements of Color.* New York: Van Nostrand Reinhold, 1970.

Sharpe, Deborah. *The Psychology of Color and Design.* Totowa, NJ: Littlefield, Adams, 1975.

Chapter 7
Looking Closer

Archer, Michael. *Art Since 1960.* London: Thames and Hudson, 2002.

Heller, Steven and Veronique Vienne, eds. *Citizen Designer: Perspectives on Design Responsibility.* New York: Allworth, 2003.

Mirzoeff, Nicholas, ed. *The Visual Culture Reader,* 2nd edition. London: Routledge, 2003.

Robertson, Jean. *Themes of Contemporary Art: Visual Art after 1980.* New York: Oxford University Press, 2005.

Sandhaus, Louise, ed. *New Media, New Narratives?* Chicago: American Center for Design, 2000.

Sollins, Susan. *Art 21: Art in the 21st Century.* New York: Henry N. Abrams, 2005.

artport.whitney.org
www.designarchives.aiga.org
www.designobserver.com
www.moma.org
www.pbs.org/art21

Index

Index

Index

Index

Image Credits

Cover and chapter title pages
1 (top image)
Image and permission: Christy Matson
2
Image and permission: Mark Napier
3
Image and permission: Betty McMurry
4
Image and permission: Betty McMurry
5
Image and permission: Betty McMurry
6
Image and permission: Mark Napier
7 (bottom image)
Image and permission: Betty McMurry

Introduction
0.1
Image and permission: 7UP

1
1.1
Image and permission: Visible Earth, NASA,
http:visibleearth.nasa.gov/
1.2
Image and permission: Frank DeBose
1.3
Image and permission: Douglas Mazonowicz/
Art Resource, NY
1.4
Image and permission: Jessie Levine, © 1982
1.5
Image and permission: Concept: O. Toscani,
courtesy of United Colors of Benetton
1.6
Image and permission: April Greiman
1.7
Image and permission: Jeff Wall
1.8
Image Robert Hickerson, photographer,
University of Kansas Spencer Museum of Art;
permission: Julie Green
1.9
Image and permission: Peter Feldstein

2
2.1
Image and permission: NASA
2.2 2.3
Author
2.4
Images and permission: Author (top and
diagram) and Warren Lehrer (bottom)

2.5
Image and permission: NASA
2.6
Images: Eve S. Mosher, photographer;
permission: Eve S. Mosher,
www.highwaterline.org
2.7
Image and permission: Margo Gradeja
2.8
Image and permission: Warren Lehrer
2.9
Image: © Guerrilla Girls, Inc., 2005;
permission: © Guerrilla Girls, Inc., 2005,
www.guerrillagirls.com
2.10
Image and permission: NASA
2.11
Image and permission: Douglas Mazonowicz/
Art Resource, NY
2.12
Image and permission: Photo Researchers,
Inc., Gianni Tortolio, photographer, © 2007
2.13
Author
2.14
Image and permission: Freer Gallery of Art,
Smithsonian Institution, Washington, DC
2.15
Image and permission: The Pierpont Morgan
Library/Art Resource, NY
2.16
Author
2.17
Image and permission: Christy Matson
2.18
Image and permission: Mark Napier
2.19 2.20
Author
2.21
Image and permission: Heejin Kim
2.22
Image and permission: digital image © The
Museum of Modern Art/licensed by SCALA/
Art Resource, NY
2.23
Image and Permission: Miller Brewing
Company and Eugene Richards,
photographer
2.24
Image: Portland Art Museum, Vivian and
Gordon Gilkey Graphic Arts Collection;
Permission: Portland Art Museum and ©
Robert Rauschenberg/licensed by VAGA

Image Credits

Image Credits

5
5.1
Image and permission: America Hurrah Archive, New York
5.2
Image and permission: Author (top left) and BP (top right)
5.3
Image and permission: Author (bottom left) and Ashley Howard (bottom right)
5.4
Image and Permission: Jack Stauffacher
5.5
Image and permission: Antonio Alcala, Studio A
5.6
Image: Art Resource, NY; permission: Art Resource, NY, © 1998 Estate of Pablo Picasso/ Artists Rights Society (ARS), New York
5.7
Image and permission: Hu Hung-Shu
5.8
Image and permission: Plenum Publishing Corporation
5.9
Image and permission: Ed Fella (left) and David Handschuh (right)
5.10
Image and permission: Phil Lasansky, The Lasansky Corporation
5.11
Image and permission: Bayer Corporation
5.12
Image and permission: Schalkwijk/Art Resource, NY, © 1998 The Andy Warhol Foundation for the Visual Arts/Artists Rights Society (ARS), New York
5.13
Image and permission: The Len Lye Foundation
5.14
Image and permission: United States Library of Congress
5.15
Image and permission: Reinhold Brown Gallery, New York City
5.16
Image: Wolfgang Weingart and author (diagram); permission: Wolfgang Weingart
5.17
Image and permission: Alinari/Art Resource, NY
5.18
Image and permission: Henry Dreyfuss and Associates and Watson-Guptill

5.19
Author
5.20
Image and permission: Kerry S. Matz
5.21
Author
5.22
Image and permission: digital image © The Museum of Modern Art/licensed by SCALA/ Art Resource, NY
5.23
Author
5.24
Image and permission: APG
5.25
Author

6
6.1
Image: photography © The Art Institute of Chicago, Bequest of Sigmund E. Edelstone; permission: The Art Institute of Chicago, Artists Rights Society (ARS), New York
6.2
Image and permission: Portland Art Museum
6.3 6.4
Author
6.5
Image and permission: Wolfgang Weingart
6.6
Image and permission: John Donovan and Eric Liftin
6.7 6.8 6.9
Author
6.10
Image and permission: Armin Hofmann
6.11 6.12 6.13 6.14 6.15 6.16 6.17 6.18
Author
6.19
Image and permission: SGI
6.20
Image and permission: photography © The Art Institute of Chicago, Helen Birch Barlett Memorial Collection
6.21 6.22
Author
6.23
Image: Portland Art Museum; permission: Portland Art Museum © 1998 The Josef and Anni Albers Foundation/Artists Rights Society (ARS), New York
6.24 6.25
Author

6.26 6.27
Image and permission: Betty McMurry
6.28
Author
6.29
Image and permission: Basar Buyukkusoglu

7
7.1
Author
7.2 7.3
Image and permission: Stephen Farrell
7.4 7.5 7.6 7.7 7.8
Image and permission: Julie Green
7.9 7.10 7.11 7.12 7.13 7.14
Image and permission: Hu Hung-Shu
7.15 7.16 7.17 7.18 7.19 7.20
Image and permission: Christy Matson
7.21 7.22 7.23
Image and permission: Morningstar, Inc.
7.24 7.25
Image and permission: Mark Napier
7.26 7.27 7.28 7.29 7.30
Image and permission: Jack Stauffacher
7.31 7.32 7.33 7.34 7.35
Image and permission: Peter Feldstein

Timeline
1
Image: photography © The Art Institute of Chicago, Wirt D. Walker Endowment; permission: The Art Institute of Chicago, licensed by VAGA
2
Image: photography © The Art Institute of Chicago, gift of Peggy Guggenheim; permission: The Art Institute of Chicago
3
Image and permission: United States Library of Congress
4
Image and permission: Mrs. Marion S. Rand
5
Image: Portland Art Museum, Vivian and Gordon Gilkey Center for Graphic Arts; permission: Portland Art Museum and © Robert Rauschenberg/licensed by VAGA
6
Image and permission: Wolfgang Weingart
7
Image and permission: Jeff Keedy
8
Image and permission: Mark Napier